MW01146144

Jeju Island

Reaching to the Core of Beauty

KOREA ESSENTIALS No. 5

Jeju Island: Reaching to the Core of Beauty

Copyright © 2011 by The Korea Foundation

All Rights Reserved.
No part of this book may be reproduced or utilized in any form
or by any means without the written permission of the publisher.

First Published in 2011 by Seoul Selection
B1 Korean Publishers Association Bldg., 105-2 Sagan-dong,
Jongno-gu, Seoul 110-190, Korea
Phone: (82-2) 734-9567
Fax: (82-2) 734-9562
Email: publisher@seoulselection.com
Website: www.seoulselection.com

ISBN: 978-89-91913-83-7   04080
ISBN: 978-89-91913-70-7   (set)
Printed in the Republic of Korea

Jeju Island

Reaching to the Core of Beauty

KOREA **KF**
FOUNDATION
한국국제교류재단

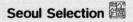

Seoul Selection

CONTENTS

Appendix

Delving Deeper

INTRODUCTION

Jeju is an island of mystery.

Most Koreans today think of Jeju as "Honeymoon Island" or "the Hawaii of Korea," projecting their fantasies onto what they imagine to be a tropical paradise. As many confess to having been there only once or not at all, it remains for the mainland an island of mystery. Steeped in mythology, shamanic ritual, and legend, with a dialect so distinct from the language of the mainland that linguists question whether it represents a separate language entirely, this "island of 18,000 gods" does its part to provide an aura of otherworldliness.

Now the recipient of UNESCO designation in three categories of natural science, the location of the World Conservation Congress in 2012, a test bed for numerous environmental soundness initiatives, and a finalist in the international New 7 Wonders of Nature campaign, Jeju is also renowned for its ecology. Forged by volcanic activity, the island has a wealth of natural phenomena and a 5,000-year history of human civilization in harmony with nature.

The "Jeju woman" is legendary for her image of strength. Originating with a unique creation myth centered on a giant goddess figure and personified by the famed diving women, Jeju has a longstanding matrifocal and economically egalitarian tradition. An island of villages, Jeju boasts a strong sense of community that has been promoted by a history of struggle for subsistence and against multiple invasions and tragedies.

Jeju is equally well known for its "three abundances"—wind, stone, and women—and for its "three absences"—beggars, thieves, and locks. Having also established itself as an island of longevity, with centenarian records kept for the past 300 years and legends circulating in ancient China about an elixir of immortality to be found here, Jeju may house another mystery: the key to eternal life. At the very least, life on this island would seem to contribute to well-being.

Outside of Korea, Jeju remains a mystery largely because so very little has been written about it in English. This book seeks to rectify that dearth of information, and to share the wonders of Jeju Island with the world.

"There is a certain melancholy about the island. We don't know where it comes from, but the feeling holds you. Perhaps it's the wind, and the grayish green tint that impregnates everything, the rocks, the tree trunks, the springs and even the sea. In Jeju, that feeling is even stronger than usual. You're at the edge of the world, as they say. At the door between the infiniteness of the Pacific Ocean and the vastness of the most extensive and populous continent on the planet. A door or a mural."

J. M. G. Le Clézio
Nobel Laureate in Literature
GEO Magazine France, March, 2009

Chapter One

ISLAND OF TREASURES

Jeju greets visitors with its unique landscape and a distinctive ocean scent for each season. The towering summit of Mt. Halla (1,950m) is visible from anywhere on the island, while the fragrance of the surrounding sea is always adrift on the wind.

The island's volcanic activity created its landmark *oreum* (parasitic cones), as well as its fields and coastline. Strangely shaped stones stimulate the imagination. These rocks have been used to create Jeju Stone Park on a site measuring some 300 hectares. At this park, with its display of rare stones and relevant artifacts, one can experience the myths and legends behind the island's abundance of stone. It presents aspects of the local stone culture beyond the familiar rock walls found all over the island.

Korea's largest island, Jeju forms a roughly oval shape stretching 75 kilometers from east to west and 41 kilometers, at its widest, from north to south. It is located off the southernmost coast of Korea, lying between China and Japan. The four seasons are distinct, though the climate is mild. The temperature rarely falls below freezing in winter, except at the summit of Mt. Halla.

With Mt. Halla at its center, the island is a treasure trove of subtropical, temperate, and even polar plant life, and a paradise for butterflies and insects. It is a habitat for several thousand species of plants and animals. Various types of seeds have been carried to the island by the Kuroshio Current and Taiwan Warm Current, among them the Poison Bulb, which is native to Africa but can be found growing on the Jeju coast.

The largest island in Korea, Jeju forms a roughly oval shape stretching 75 kilometers from east to west and 41 kilometers, at its widest, from north to south. It is located off the southernmost coast of Korea, lying between China and Japan.

Spring: A field of rape flowers in full bloom in front of Mt. Sanbang

Summer: Hamdeok Beach

Autumn: A field full of cosmos flowers

Winter: Snow covers the flanks of Mt. Halla

Jeju, Through a Poet's Eyes

The black mountain ridges writhe. Clusters of *oreum* awaken, ready to gather and rush off somewhere. This is the break of dawn on Jeju.

The wind and light live together on Yongnuni Oreum. Pure white Grass-of-Parnassus flowers sway to and fro. The fields are filled with wildflowers. People call these rolling hills bulging up out of the flat land by the name of "*oreum*." Jeju Island is home to more of these parasitic cones than anywhere else in the world. You could climb one a day for a year and still have more to see.

Here and there, the larger *oreum* include modest traditional tombs, surrounded by stone walls. Here, it seems, that the end of one life is the beginning of another. The stone figures of young boys, covered with the moss of ages, have become friends of the deceased. Those who made the statues and carved the sublime expressions that capture the happiness and sadness of humanity are now among the nameless inhabitants of the island.

From afar come the calls of a herder rounding up his horses.

Oreum at sunrise

Manse Hill on Mt. Halla, surrounded by a sea of clouds

Cows roam about, grazing on the meadows. The *oreum* are home to vegetable gardens offering bracken, wild greens, medicinal herbs, and comfort to the weary. These age-old landforms were strongholds during the struggles of the island people, and a resting place for those who had lived out their lives.

The wind on the *oreum* does not slumber easily. It is delectable, filled with the salty scent of the sea. Climb up to the top of an *oreum* and look out at the vast open sea and Mt. Halla. The winding ridges of the mountain and its surrounding *oreum*, the rounded thatched-roof houses and the coastline, the valleys, the meandering stone walls around the fields, the round tombs—Jeju is a land of graceful curves.

Near Yongnuni Oreum you can find Darangshwi Oreum, the queen of them all. On a bright, moonlit night, the moon is cradled in its crater. The *oreum* is like a woman's ample breasts, like women lying down or hunkered over. The deep, sunken craters are the wombs of the earth, containing all creation and all destruction.

Jeju is a land of light. The light and wind atop an *oreum* create

At 1,324 meters, Sara Oreum is the highest of Jeju Island's 386 *oreum*. A mysterious lake is hidden in its crater. Sara Oreum was opened to the general public in the autumn of 2010. It was the first of the 40 *oreum* in Mt. Halla National Park to be opened.

unimaginable color. The photographer Kim Young Gap was so enraptured by this incredibly dazzling light that after a visit he ended up settling here. For a long time, he would gaze out mesmerized by the light of the *oreum* and the light of the earth that flowed over Yongnuni.

The road to Sara Oreum, which passes Sanjeong Lake, is the way to Mt. Halla. One path up the mountain, beginning at Seongpanak, sparkles with the crimson of maples, the green of broadleaf trees, and the bright red of kamatsuka berries. For the residents of Jeju, Mt. Halla is a life force as well as the foundation of their imagination. Seen from above, it is like a plush carpet. Halla is the peak from which one can reach out and touch the Milky Way. As you lie down in her crater and look up at the heavens, the stars come pouring down. It is a mountain of myth, a maternal mountain—and a lonely mountain, but one that comforts all who come within its sturdy embrace. It is a mountain that stands up to typhoons and to external pressure, protecting all those in need of comfort.

KIM YOUNG GAP

In 1985, a young photographer relocated from Seoul to Jeju with a plan to remain for two or three years as he photographed the island. Kim Young Gap soon became obsessed in his quest to discover the "hidden beauty"—the "flesh" and "bones"—of Jeju's landscape. This coupled with his own deeply felt connection to the island's natural environment ("My being becomes grass, trees, insects; I am assimilated into their life") and he would not leave the island, until his untimely death from a degenerative disease in 2005. According to his wishes, his body was cremated and his ashes scattered beneath a persimmon tree (once struck by lightning) that stands at the entrance to his final Jeju home.

A unique feature of Kim's process was his technique of returning to the same location day after day, sometimes for months on end, in order to achieve the best possible portrayal—in terms of the interplay of light and shadow, the relationship between sky and land, or some ineffable quality that only he could sense. He also took photographs of the same location in contrasting seasons, displaying them together in order to indicate the

changeable nature of the land. He integrated the elements—fog, rain, clouds, wind, sunlight—into his art, even including the raindrops that fell on his lens.

Park Hyun-il, Kim's former student and longtime friend who continues to manage the gallery in which Kim's art is housed, says "He became one with the beauty he sought." Kim encouraged others to experience his work with the same heartfelt connection, and thus refused to name his photographs in order to allow for a unique impression on the part of each viewer.

Kim produced some of the most remarkable photographs of Jeju to date, displaying his deep understanding of and relationship to this island. Yongnuni and Darangshi Oreum were among his favorite subjects.

With numerous exhibitions and two posthumously published books about his work, he is celebrated, along with painters Lee Jung Seop and Byun Shi-ji, as one of Jeju's greatest artists.

Gallery Dumoak, a former elementary school converted into Kim's final studio and home, now displays much of his work. "Dumoak" is one of the old names for Mt. Halla. The gallery is located in a rural area near Samdal Village, south of Seongsan Ilchulbong in the easternmost part of Jeju.

Gallery Dumoak, a former elementary school converted into Kim's final studio and home, now displays much of his work.

Think of what can be found there. Large boulders embrace the trees, and the trees embrace the boulders. These places where rocks and trees intertwine are called *gotjawal*. They are primeval forests, manifesting Jeju's unspoiled character. Nowhere is the wilderness instinct stronger than in Jeju, a volcanic island that burst forth in a pillar of flame two million years ago. The swift yet steady lava has left its traces everywhere. Camellia Hill in Seonheulgot also bears the mark of fire. This *gotjawal* is a treasure trove that evokes the essence of life. It is here that the lives and history of the people of Jeju have been shaped. Here, they made charcoal, picked berries, and cut down trees to build homes, in a forest sheltering all sorts of rare plants, roe deer, and other living things.

So it is with the path up Geomun Oreum. This ancient forest speaks: "You humans are part of nature, too, and so you should adopt the ways of nature." It tells us to be humble. Here we must walk more slowly, working our way along the forest path with our heads bowed respectfully.

A geological park is Jeju, a single dot on the sea. Unlike the Mediterranean or other oceans, the sea here cries out with

The volcanic island of Jeju is also famous for its dense forests. Forests are filled with life, supporting a huge variety of organisms.
Wild roe deer live in Mt. Halla National Park (top).
Gwaneumsa Trail, in Mt. Halla National Park, is reminiscent of primeval forest (bottom).

all its being. How can the color of the water look so different from one village to another? It changes from indigo to sapphire, deep blue, and even inky black.

On a day thick with fog, the melancholy melody of a shaman's song drifts plaintively on the Jeju seas. The song has a more somber tone than even the black rocks of Jeju. It is the sound of prayers for the souls of those lost at sea, and for the well-being of those who rely on the sea. In the second lunar month, Grandmother Yeongdeung, the wind goddess, arrives on the breeze. Jeju is a paradise for 18,000 deities. Mt. Halla, the ocean, caves, every village—all are permeated with mythic roots. As if to speak for this kingdom of the gods, each village maintains a shrine, where the villagers perform rituals.

1
2
3

The sea around Jeju Island differs in color from region to region.
1. Hyeopjae Beach 2. Sagye Beach 3. Yongmeori tuff ring and cliffs

The beauty of the island has been created by the wind and the waves. Beyond Soesokkak, in Seogwipo, the coastlines of Oedolgae and Daepo-ri and the seaside cliffs of Yerae-dong draw exclamations of wonderment. They were born of Jeju's volcanic creation. They are the traces of lava flows stopped in their tracks. The land of the volcano, Jeju is an island of fire, its stones carved into layers and marked by the wind. They are the masterpieces of the gods, shaped by the wind and the waves.

It is exhilarating to stand before the stone pillars (*jusangjeolli*) that rise straight up out of the ocean. Long, long ago, when the volcano erupted, it spewed forth molten lava. That lava writhed and flowed like a red river down to the ocean, its tears stopping as soon as it met the water. The power of the lava produced such celebrated natural attractions as Mt. Halla, the lava caves of Geomun Oreum, and Seongsan Ilchulbong, or "Sunrise Peak".

Daepo Jusangjeolli, black hexagonal stone pillars piled on top of each other. They unfold like a folding screen as if a god elaborately piled up blocks of stone.

The entire island is a geological park. There are stone cairns, stone dikes, tomb embankments, salt fields. Riddled with holes, the basalt is filled with the wind. The people of old cut these rocks and shaped them into the items they used in everyday life.

Volcanic formations in the shape of all sorts of animals, rocks with faces like people, and the age-old folklore of Jeju: the place to experience these things is the Jeju Stone Park. This is a garden of myth imbued with the legend of Grandmother Seolmundae, the giantess who created Jeju Island, and her of 500 sons. Time there flows slowly, like the lava itself. Those in a hurry would be better off not stopping by.

The splendor of Seongsan Ilchulbong is not to be missed, offering such a magnificent sunrise that people pay homage to the breathtaking scene. A mountain that exploded out of the ocean! It is even more graceful when seen from a distance, rather than up close; its majesty is greater when seen from above.

So why do sad eyes gaze upon the rugged coastline of Seongsan Ilchulbong? To gain a true picture of Jeju, you have to learn about its scars. Only then will you realize why this island, covered with brilliant yellow rape flowers under the

Measuring 180m in height, Seongsan Ilchulbong is a tuff cone formed by hydrovolcanic activity in shallow seas around 5,000 years ago. It arose from the accumulation of volcanic ash during a violent reaction between hot magma from underground and seawater (top).

Visitors to Jeju Stone Park can see works of art made by the volcanoes themselves (bottom).

Seongsan Ilchulbong, a designated UNESCO World Natural Heritage Site, seen from the air

spring sunshine, is so entrancing, why the camellia flowers are even redder than its once molten lava.

Jeju Island has withstood various upheavals. Such was the fate of an island located in the center of Northeast Asia. On the coast of Seongsan Ilchulbong is a series of cave openings. These are the Jinji Caves, dating from the Japanese colonial period. The people forced to carve out these openings were the powerless residents of Jeju.

Six decades ago, the island was caught in the vortex of the April 3rd Uprising (1948–1954), a tragedy of modern Korean history. One of the bloodiest incidents rooted in the ideological clash between the left and right after liberation from Japan, the uprising led to a horrendous loss of human life between April 1948 and the winter of 1949. At one time, countless refugees sought shelter on Mt. Halla. None of the wondrous sights of the island was spared the carnage. The Jeju April 3rd Peace Park is dedicated to their memory.

The road to Mt. Songak is also steeped in the winds of that history. Even today, hangars built during the Japanese colonial period hug the ground with their gaping maws. Sesal Oreum is marred by scars of the 1948 uprising. If you stop and lower your head, you might hear the work songs of those who endured a harrowing life here on this dry and crumbling volcanic ash soil, long trapped in nature.

Finally, we arrive at wind-swept Mt. Songak. From here, where even the blades of grass find no rest, we can see two of Jeju's brother islands, Gapado and Marado. (To see more pristine islands, you must depart from Jeju.) Within Jeju's territory, we also find the islands of Biyangdo, Chujado, and Udo, along with numerous islets.

The tomb of an infant at Neobeunsungi, an April 3rd historic site. Government punitive forces slaughtered even children during the incident. In Korea, the graves of children do not have headstones.

The sorrows of Jeju Island can be traced back to the Joseon era. To the locals, Jeju was simply a harsh, arid land—a lonely island where even the little residents had would be plundered by Japanese pirates from time to time. The Joseon Dynasty (1392–1910) used Jeju for a place of exile; the punishment for felons who escaped the death penalty was exile to Jeju. But with the exquisite scenic beauty of the island, the isolation of the exiles was sublimated into art. A notable example is Kim Jeong-hui, a late Joseon scholar and celebrated calligrapher, who was forced to live in exile on Jeju for nine years after falling afoul of political intrigues.

At twilight, the *oreum* turn back into sleeping black mountain ridges. At Chagwido, the glow of the setting sun is bewitching. As you stand atop Suwolbong, a world geological park at the western end of Jeju, the setting sun seems to question you—about the life you have lived, the life you are going to live, and what it is you have lost.

Jeju fills visitors with wonder at the beauty they are constantly encountering. The sunset toward Chagwido, as seen from Suwolbong is one of Jeju's top sights.

To heal yourself, then, and to find inspiration in your life, throw everything aside and come to this island. You will feel its vibrant energy. Wherever you look on Jeju, your eyes meet the horizon, Mt. Halla, and the *oreum*. The twisting Olle trails, Saryeoni Woodland Path, coastal routes, stone ways... those who have walked these paths know just how blessed Korea is to have Jeju Island. It draws no attention to itself yet possesses all forms of beauty: a symphony of the south, a land of rapture and sorrow that has survived through wind and rain.

The people of Jeju have cultivated the rough, dry landscape where they live in order to feed themselves, creating beautiful landscapes in the process. Here, a snow-covered Mt. Halla is seen from the green tea field of Dosun.

Manse Hill on Mt. Halla filled with azaleas

THE "TRIPLE CROWN" OF UNESCO
NATURAL SCIENCE DESIGNATIONS

Jeju has been awarded the "triple crown" of UNESCO designations for natural sciences—Bioreserve, World Natural Heritage, and Geopark. It is the first place in the world to achieve this.

In 2002, Mt. Halla and part of the Seogwipo coastline were declared a biosphere reserve, totaling 44% of the island's surface area. It was later upgraded to include the whole of Jeju Island.

Five years later, in 2007, "World Natural Heritage" status was bestowed upon Halla's nature reserve; the title was given to Mt. Halla, the Geomun

Autumn on Yeongsil Trail, Mt. Halla

Spring on Yeongsil Trail, Mt. Halla

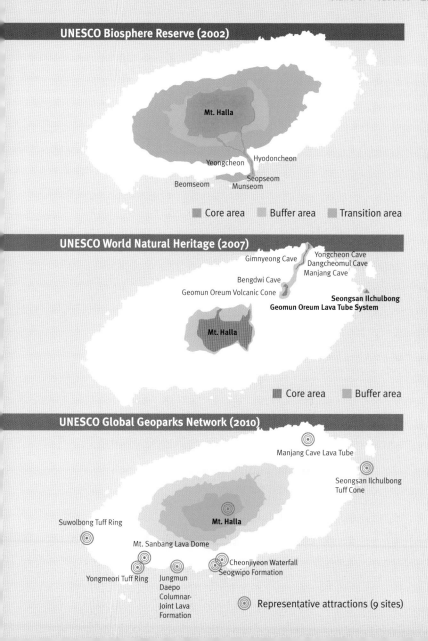

UNESCO Biosphere Reserve (2002)

Mt. Halla

Yeongcheon   Hyodoncheon

Beomseom   Seopseom
Munseom

■ Core area   ■ Buffer area   ■ Transition area

UNESCO World Natural Heritage (2007)

Yongcheon Cave
Dangcheomul Cave
Gimnyeong Cave   Manjang Cave

Bengdwi Cave
Geomun Oreum Volcanic Cone

Seongsan Ilchulbong
Geomun Oreum Lava Tube System

Mt. Halla

■ Core area   ■ Buffer area

UNESCO Global Geoparks Network (2010)

Manjang Cave Lava Tube

Seongsan Ilchulbong
Tuff Cone

Suwolbong Tuff Ring   Mt. Halla

Mt. Sanbang Lava Dome

Cheonjiyeon Waterfall
Seogwipo Formation
Yongmeori Tuff Ring   Jungmun
Daepo
Columnar-   Representative attractions (9 sites)
Joint Lava
Formation

(pronounced "guh-moon") Oreum system of lava tubes, and the Seongsan Ilchulbong tuff cone.

The most recent recognition by UNESCO came in December 2010, when the entire island was designated a "geopark" and included in the Global Geoparks Network. In addition to the three sites previously noted (specifically Manjang Cave in the Geomun Oreum lava tube system), six more were identified: the Suwolbong tuff ring, Mt. Sanbang lava dome, Yongmeori tuff ring and cliffs, Jungmun Daepo columnar-joint lava formation ("Daepo Jusangjeolli"), Seogwipo Formation, and Cheonjiyeon Falls.

Of particular note is the fact that Mt. Halla has been designated in all three of UNESCO's natural science categories. One of the Korean people's three most sacred mountains (the others are Mt. Jiri in the southern region of the peninsula, and Mt. Baekdu in the north), it is especially holy to the people of Jeju Island. Halla is the island's progenitor, the physical manifestation of a giant goddess called Seolmundae, the "mother" of nearly 400 secondary volcanic cones ("*oreum*") perceived by the people of Jeju as kin, and a site of rich biodiversity. Overseeing all of Jeju as a benign ancestor, Halla's significance to this island culture that cannot be overstated.

The benefit of these recognitions by UNESCO are not only ecological but economic and social as well. Direct social and ecological applications can be found in educational and preservation initiatives. As Jeju enjoys an enhancement of its image through such designations, the tourism and MICE (meetings, incentives, conferencing, and exhibitions) industries also benefit. Jeju's ability to obtain funding, from both domestic and international sources, increases exponentially. The island's branding of products for export is also enhanced.

A hidden social benefit is found in the increased value societies place on their resources following external recognition of same. One doesn't always know what one has... until someone else points it out.

Jeju has additionally been afforded recognition by the Ramsar Convention for three wetlands "of international importance": Mulyeongari Oreum (2006), Muljangori Oreum (2008), and 1100 Altitude (2010).

Following the recent Geopark designation, Jeju government is organizing "geo-tours" with trained "geo-guides" and is considering other ways to welcome visitors to these sites.

Mulyeongari Oreum, a site designated in 2006 as a Wetland of International Importance by the Ramsar Convention on Wetlands (top) Yongcheon Cave, part of the Geomun Oreum Lava Tube System, designated in 2007 by UNESCO as a World Natural Heritage Site (bottom)

Berit Stream on Jeju Olle Trail Route 8

Jeju Olle

A system of hiking trails, the brainchild of Jeju native and former journalist Suh Myung Sook, very nearly encircles the island. Twenty-four trails have been formed to date, three of them on the outlying islands of Udo, Chujado, and Gapado, and the project is scheduled to complete the circumscribing of Jeju by 2013.

"Olle" refers to a path from road to house in the traditional Jeju village. The word is also a homonym for another meaning, "Are you coming?" or "Will you come?" which represents the invitation of Jeju Olle. Inspired by her 2006 trek on the renowned Camino de Santiago trail in western Europe, Suh has created this system of trails as a gift to her homeland. As a result, she has changed the very nature of Korean tourism.

Jeju Olle is now the most popular attraction on the island, and despite what early naysayers—including the local government—predicted,

Olle Trail Map

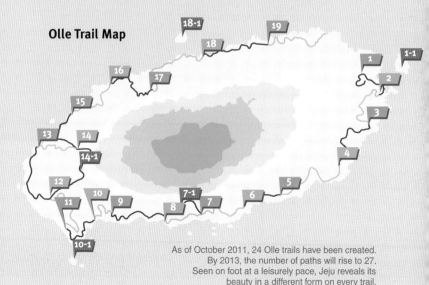

As of October 2011, 24 Olle trails have been created. By 2013, the number of paths will rise to 27. Seen on foot at a leisurely pace, Jeju reveals its beauty in a different form on every trail.

Korean tourists have come out en masse to seek out these trails. Typically focused on short, intense, guided group tours, Koreans have discovered the joys of walking an average of 15 kilometers over four to six hours while immersed in nature. The sociological impact on this harried post-war nation cannot be overstated.

Olle trails Nos. 7 and 8, which pass along the breathtakingly scenic southern shore of the island and connect with one another near Seogwipo, are the most popular by a margin. Walking along these trails, one can view sights such as Oedolgae, Daepo Jusangjeolli, Jungmun Beach, and much more.

An annual Walking Festival began in 2010 and now takes place every

November over four days and four Olle trails. In conjunction with this event, Jeju Olle hosts the World Trail Conference, drawing experts from eight other countries across the globe, each of which has its own famous trail. It is the goal of the Jeju Olle Foundation to fully include this system among the world's greatest trails, a title already bestowed upon it by the world-renowned "Lonely Planet" guidebooks.

"Koreans are driven by fresh memories of war and extreme poverty," Suh says. "My hope is that Jeju Olle can help us to slow down, enjoy nature, and interact with fellow travelers and locals in a more humane way."

The Jeju Olle office is located on the coast in Seogwipo, and Olle information is readily available at the airport and all major tourist sites.

1	2	
---	---	6
3	4	5

1. Seongsanpo gil,
Jeju Olle Trail Route 1

2. Dombenang gil,
Jeju Olle Trail Route 7

3. Seogwipo Seaside,
Jeju Olle Trail Route 6

4. Soesokkak,
Jeju Olle Trail Route 6

5. Jonmosal Beach,
Jeju Olle Trail Route 8

6. Teukjeonsa supgil,
Jeju Olle Trail Route 13

Chapter Two

ISLAND OF NATURE

The island of Jeju juts up abruptly off the southern tip of the Korean Peninsula. Stretching from east to west like a yam with Mt. Halla soaring majestically from its center, the island looks from a distance like an open parasol. Halla is the second tallest mountain in Korea, after Mt. Baekdu to the north. A long-dormant volcano, Halla seems like a single mass of basalt forming an entire island. With the mountain standing so high above the sea, one can only imagine how high it must actually be from the ocean floor.

The Jeju Folklore and Natural History Museum in Jeju, the island's largest city, features an exhibit of the chemically preserved bones of a red bear. Discovered in Billemot Cave in Aewol in Township, the site of the earliest known settlers of this island, the bones of the animal (which is known to inhabit only northern polar regions) strongly suggest that the island was once part of the mainland. The volcano that became Mt. Halla likely erupted between the third and forth ice age, causing the area adjoining the mainland to sink into the sea while the remaining areas became elevated.

Due to this volcanic activity, Jeju has numerous rock and natural caves. Manjang is a lava cave in Gimnyeong, a village in Gujwa Township about 30 minutes east of Jeju City. It is 6.8 kilometers in length, making it the world's largest lava tube. About 13 meters high and 15 meters wide, this magnificent cave is actually a tunnel that was formed by lava flowing from Mt. Halla. A number of bizarrely distorted stalagmites indicate that the cave is still evolving. The Gimnyeong cave is tied to the legend of Magistrate Seo Ryeon who valiantly battled and killed a giant serpent that lived in the cave and harassed the local villagers. On the ceiling of the cave, one can still see marks resembling the scales of a serpent.

The Manjang and Gimnyeong caves are on the eastern side of the island. Along the island's western side is another cluster of caves

Entrance to Manjang Cave, designated a UNESCO World Natural Heritage Site in 2007 and recognized as a UNESCO Geopark

that includes Hyeopjae and Ssangyong. The entire area around these two caves is open to tourists. In addition to these, the island includes a large number of subterranean caves that are not open to the public, including the previously mentioned Billemot. These caves, and their surrounding areas, are protected as Natural Monument No. 236.

Lava column, Manjang Cave

Map of Lava Tube

Gimnyeong Cave ◎   ◎ Yongcheon Cave
Bengdwi Cave ◎   ◎ Dangcheomul Cave
Manjang Cave ◎

◎ Billemot Cave

◎
Hyeopjae & Ssangyong Cave

DEFINED BY NATURE

Jeju Island has always been defined by nature. An ecological wonder in the comprehensiveness of its geologic features, a place in which humans and nature have co-existed harmoniously for millennia, a temperate island with flora and fauna from both polar and subtropical regions, a finalist in the global New 7 Wonders of Nature campaign, and a site that has now been given more nature-related UNESCO designations than any other on earth, Jeju is nothing if not rich in natural capital.

Jeju's inhabitants have also historically struggled with nature and the elements to maintain their existence. The indigenous people of this island culture combined hunter-gatherer and agrarian ways, developing multiple methods for harnessing the natural features of the island and for coping with the hardships of its climate and geography. Created by volcanic eruption, the island is over 90% basalt which rendered efforts at agriculture nearly impossible. With strong winds owing to its location at sea and multiple seasonal typhoons, plus perpetual drought conditions from living atop porous rock with no means of accessing the aquifers below, life on this island has

Jeju Island was formed from basalt due to volcanic eruptions. As a result, its ground does not hold water well. In the past, the people of Jeju suffered from constant water shortages.

been challenging to say the least.

Nevertheless, the people of what is now known as Jeju did not simply prevail; they became ingenious in their efforts to develop the best possible ways to cope with what was considered a harsh environment. What's more, as with all animistic early peoples, they looked to nature for spiritual sustenance and developed a multitude of myths and legends with which they comforted themselves in their difficulties.

Jeju artists of the past and present, have repeatedly focused on the island's landscape and elements as a defining force of the people themselves, and their gods.

The first UNESCO designation given to this island, typically identified as "bioreserve," is part of the "Man and the Biosphere Programme." This is to say, it specifically recognizes the

Farmland swept away by heavy rains (top)
Stony ground and a lack of water have made hard workers of the people of Jeju. They built walls from the stone and cleared and cultivated the land (bottom).

harmony between members of a longstanding human civilization and the ecological system in which they reside. The second designation, World Natural Heritage, identifies a natural site or structure as particularly significant to the "common heritage of humanity"—once again linking the two.

Of course, humans are not separate from their biosphere; we are one element of it, however distanced we may feel ourselves to be. This interrelatedness—indeed, interdependence—among species in a closed ecological system is something which indigenous peoples inherently understand, and the early people of Jeju were no

A green tea field (top)
Rape is sometimes grown and eaten as a vegetable. It has now become the flower that represents spring on Jeju Island (bottom).

exception. They found creative ways of living in oneness with the natural world, no matter how much hardship it brought them. This is evidenced by their many inventive agricultural and marine practices, building methods, means for clothing themselves, and other subsistence techniques. They also practiced stewardship, using only what they needed and replacing it as they did so. Like indigenous peoples everywhere, they lived a form of deep ecology that modern civilizations have long forgotten and are now struggling to recreate.

The people of Jeju have always lived, both literally and metaphorically, in the shadow of Mt. Halla. It is their progenitor—both in the volcanic activity that created this island and in the mythology of a giant grandmother goddess called Seolmundae, the personification of the central mountain so sacred to the people of Jeju.

"Jeju's nature is feminine," says Jeju Olle founder and chairperson Suh Myung Sook, a sentiment echoed by many—and manifested daily by the famed diving women, who represent an innate form of eco-feminism.

FORGED BY FIRE, TURNED TO STONE

"Jeju is Halla, and Halla is Jeju." A longstanding saying among the island's people, this perfectly expresses their relationship with its central figure.

There is perhaps no more dramatic creator than an erupting volcano. As fire and ash spews from above and torrents of burning lava from below quickly turn to stone, all with great energy and force, the resulting topography is inevitably exaggerated.

Jeju's natural wonders are a stunning example. With eruptions beginning as early as 2 million years ago, it was a final major explosion that took place between 400,000 and 700,000 years ago that formed the Jeju Island we see today.

The originating force at the center of it all is Mt. Halla, a shield

Baengnokdam, a lake at the summit of Mt. Halla.
Mt. Halla is the highest mountain not only on Jeju but anywhere in the Republic of Korea.

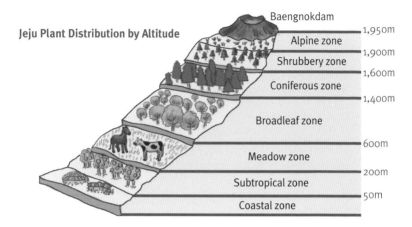

Jeju Plant Distribution by Altitude

Baengnokdam

1,950m
Alpine zone
1,900m
Shrubbery zone
1,600m
Coniferous zone
1,400m
Broadleaf zone
600m
Meadow zone
200m
Subtropical zone
50m
Coastal zone

volcano whose slopes represent a temperate climate and ecosystem all its own. From base to peak, the distinct flora zones of this 1,950m structure are: coastal, subtropical, meadow, broadleaf tree, coniferous, shrub, alpine, and finally the peak with a crater that houses a crystal-clear lake and is home to many more species of flora and fauna. Both polar and subtropical species are found in this mountain ecosystem.

Parallel to Mt. Halla are the *oreum*—nearly 400 of them. These smaller mountains, most of them merely hills, are the most distinctive characteristic of the island and represent the largest cluster, or colony, of secondary volcanic cones anywhere in the world. Although they are all called *oreum* by Jeju's people, there are cinder and scoria cones, lava domes, and more than 20 tuff cones and rings among those by the sea.

In addition to the crater atop Halla, with its magnificent lake Baengnokdam, Jeju is home to several other distinguished craters, providing further evidence of the island's volcanic origins. Indeed, most of the *oreum* are topped with craters. Notable examples are

Oreum

the one that tops Seongsan Ilchulbong, another of Jeju's UNESCO-designated sites; one at the peak of Abu Oreum, with a semicircle of trees and a population of horses; and Sangumburi, a crater found not on a cone but at ground level.

Volcanic Jeju also has caves and lava tubes dotting the island. There are more than 120 of the latter, though only a few are open to the public. The lava tube at Manjang Cave in Geomun Oreum, designated by UNESCO as a World Natural Heritage and Geopark site, is the largest of its kind in the world. In actuality, Geomun Oreum

The summit of Seongsan Ilchulbong, measuring 182 meters high (top)

Geomun Oreum, a designated UNESCO World Natural Heritage Site (bottom)

Coastal roads

The Coastal Roads provide a good way of enjoying Jeju's spectacular volcanic delights.

Circumscribing the island is Ring Road, also called Ocean Road, Coast or Coastal Road, and Shore Road—and known officially as Route 12. Drivers would do well to watch for the road signs, as the course makes some unexpected turns. Traversing the shoreline much of the time, this route affords drivers some stunning scenery of the sea, harbors, and seaside villages, as well as many of the natural wonders of Jeju.

Beginning in the east at Yongduam (Dragon Head) Rock and extending several kilometers to the west, the capital city's Coastal Road is dotted with restaurants, cafés, and pensions. Seaside dining, with outdoor plastic tables and chairs at the water's edge in summertime and food at reasonable prices, can be found at the east end of this stretch in Yongdam-dong. As one drives further west, the restaurants become more decidedly upscale, and small pensions offer accommodations with breathtaking views of the sea.

houses nine caves and an entire lava tube system, thought to be between 100,000 and 300,000 years old.

Several outlying islands and numerous islets surround Jeju, another result of the volcanic eruptions.

The beaches along Jeju's coast are a myriad of colors—some white, others gray, still others black, pink, and beige, with the water changing color from site to site as well. Along the beaches are such spectacular volcanic delights as Seongsan Ilchulbong, the Seogwipo Formation, the Daepo Jusangjeolli (Columnar Joints), Oedolgae Rock, the Yongmeori Cliffs, Mt. Songak, and Suwolbong. The basalt that makes up the vast majority of this island including these stunning formations, has nevertheless been a great source of difficulty. Its soil is too rocky for farming, and it is poor at retaing

A popular option among visitors is to rent a car and drive this road, which can be accomplished in a single day—although it is more enjoyable if you allow time to make many stops along the way. Traveling by bicycle or scooter is also popular, although as a matter of precaution, one is advised to keep in mind that car drivers are more often looking at the sights than the road.

The route can also traveled by bus: the East Belt Line and West Belt Line buses each cover half of the Ring Road, traversing between Jeju City and Seogwipo along the coast of the eastern and western halves of the island, respectively.

groundwater due to its porous nature and deep aquifers. On it grows an ancient rainforest (known locally as *gotjawal*) that covers more than 12% of the island.

Gotjawal: THE LUNGS OF JEJU

In the native language of Jeju, the word *gotjawal* simply refers to any forest that grows out of rocky terrain and presents a virtually impassible mixture of trees and undergrowth. There are several such areas on the island, mostly on the middle slopes of Mt. Halla, with two each in the extreme eastern and western regions. Collectively, they cover 224km², or 55,000 acres (22,258 hectares). The *gotjawal* are referred to as the "lungs of Jeju." Indeed, it is well recognized that they are essential to the carbon cycle, or the oxygen-carbon dioxide exchange necessary for an ecosystem.

Additionally, this forested land is critical for Jeju's groundwater supply system. Helping to capture rainwater in its canopy, the forest redirects the fresh water, which is then filtered through extensive

Map of Jeju's *Gotjawal*

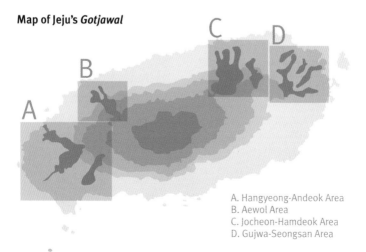

A. Hangyeong-Andeok Area
B. Aewol Area
C. Jocheon-Hamdeok Area
D. Gujwa-Seongsan Area

layers of porous volcanic rock until it reaches the aquifers deep below the island's surface. This is a structure vital to not only the collection but also the purification and replenishment of the groundwater into a particularly pure mineral water. This forested land is also crucial for flood control and seasonal water retention or downstream conservation. Furthermore, it contributes to an underground spring system for Jeju's surface wetlands.

One unique characteristic of these forests is the shallow root system of the trees, which owes itself to the rocky base on which they sit. Age and storm can easily topple a tree, leaving it lying on the forest floor. But because of the moist nature of rainforests, the roots of the fallen trees receive enough moisture to remain alive. The tree continues to leaf and bloom, its roots wrapped around rocks.

As the *gotjawal* is, by definition, virtually inaccessible to humans, it remains a biosphere that is species-rich and pristine. The people of Jeju have a close, historically anthropomorphic relationship with these forested regions, much as they do with Mt. Halla, the many *oreum*, and other natural structures on the island, and numerous

Gotjawal, the lungs of Jeju

myths and legends center around them. They are a feature of ecological, historical, and cultural significance. They are also threatened now by development, leading to a number of governmental and civic efforts to preserve them.

RELATIONSHIP WITH WATER

As an island, Jeju is naturally surrounded by the sea. In addition, the *gotjawal* rainforest system contributes to the vast aquifer on which this island rests, as well an underground system of springs. There are several wetland regions, three of which are listed with the Ramsar Convention as being "of international importance." Jeju also has several significant waterfalls, which, like so many of the natural structures and phenomena of this island, have inspired myths and legends. A rainy season and multiple typhoons bombard the island with water.

Most of Jeju's people have always gleaned their livelihood from the sea, most notably the fishermen and diving women—indeed, all inhabitants of coastal villages have partaken in the seaside harvest of anchovies and other trapped sea creatures. While the diving women in particular made a decent living, the frequent typhoons and other storms all too often brought suffering and death. Fresh water has always been lacking at the surface due to the island's porous rock and the inability, until recently, to reach the deep aquifers—or even to know that they existed. Springs are found in a

1. Spring on Geomun Oreum
2. *Gaegasi Namu*, a member of the genus Quercus (oak), in a *gotjawal*
3. In Jeju, the basalt rock makes water storage difficult. Wetlands are both important places of water storage and valuable wildlife havens.
4. A valley at Mt. Halla

few areas, but they are relatively rare. Crater lakes are also few in number, while sources of fresh water were difficult to attain with any regularity. Dry farming was the norm; rice farming, which required wet cultivation, was considered secondary in the region, and both digging and collecting from communal wells depended upon collective effort and inspired labor songs.

The relationship between Jeju's people and its water has always been as significant as these with stone and wind.

FLORA AND FAUNA

Species of both flora and Fauna are extensively represented in a biosphere as rich as Jeju's. According to one recent source, "Jeju Volcanic Island & Lava Tubes" (2009), there are 77 species of mammals, 198 of birds, eight of reptiles and another eight of amphibians, 893 of insects, and another 74 of arachnids. More than 2,000 species of vegetation have been identified in temperate, sub-tropical, and polar categories.

Indigenous species include the Jeju weasel (*Mustela siberica quelpartis*), blackheaded snake (*Sibynophis chinensis*), Jeju salamander (*Hynobius quelpartensis*), Jeju gold beetle (*Chejuanomala quelparta*), *Abies koreana* fir, the *Sasa quelpartensis* (a plant), and fairy pitta (*Pitta branchyura*, a type of bird), among many others.

In the coastal or seasonal tidal zone of the island, halophilic plants such as reeds and mallow abound, and migratory birds can include spoonbills, swans, and storks. The evergreen broadleaf forest that constitutes the next zone has two *Cimbidium* tree species, *Cimbidium* tree species, *Ardisia japonica*, and others; examples of birds include great tits and bush warblers. The grassland zone includes marshland with such plant species as *Braseria schreberi* and *Marsilea quadrifolia* as well as tiger keelback snakes and black-spotted pond frogs. The deciduous forest region houses such tree species as *Prunus yedoensis* and *Carpinus*

1. The fairy pitta (*Pitta brachyura*), designated Natural Monument No. 204 2. Buds on an *Agave americana*, known in Korean as *yongseollan* and in English as the century plant, as it flowers once every hundred years 3. The "Jeju weasel" (*Mustela sibirica quelpartis*), an endemic subspecies of Siberian weasel 4. The *gusangjangmi beoseot (Bondarzewia montana)*, a species of fungus not yet recorded in Korea 5. *Boksucho (Adonis amurensis)* is also known as the "snow lotus" because of its resemblance to a lotus flower blooming in the snow. 6. The "Jeju badger", an indigenous species 7. *Jeju bibaribaem*

laxiflora, as well as mammals like roe deer and badgers.

Next in order of elevation is the coniferous area, which includes trees such as *Pinus densiflora* as well as shrubs like the crowberry; birds of prey like the common buzzard and peregrine falcon make this region their home. The alpine shrub zone, bordering the crater of Mt. Halla and its lake, houses many small shrub species hardy enough to withstand lower temperatures and high winds. The Jeju salamander and Korean fire-bellied toad are found in the lake itself.

Marine life also abounds in the waters around Jeju Island, including 350 species of sedentary fish and countless migratory varieties. Marine algae and mollusks are likewise prolific. More than 150 species of shellfish and an equal number of crustacean species reside in Jeju's coastal waters. Coral reef populations are found in abundance off of Jeju's southern shore, and recently have been located north of the island as well; this is assumed to be an indication of climate change.

1. Pampas grass
2. *Siromi*, a plant native to Mt. Halla
3. A flock of black cranes, migratory birds designated and protected as Natural Monument No. 228
4. Hado-ri migratory bird habitat
5. A pod of dolphins
6. A lesser frigate bird, one of the fastest species in the world
7. A family of red deer on Mt. Halla
8. Jeju's marine ecosystem

MAN AND HIS HORSE

There are three types of horses on Jeju Island: the Jeju horse (also known as a pony), international racing thoroughbreds, and the Halla horse, which is a hybrid of the two. Today, these horses are not used for military purposes, transport, or field labor; instead, they are raised for racing, recreational riding, and food.

Although horses are believed to have existed on Jeju since prehistoric times, the first record of them on the island dates back to 1073, when the ruling Mongolian Yuan Dynasty of China established a ranch on what was then Tamna in order to breed warhorses. Jeju was home to ten large horse ranches during the Joseon era. During the reign of King Sejong in the 15th century, a 200-kilometer-long stone wall, called the "*jatseong*," was built around Mt. Halla to prevent the horses from escaping. The consumption of *malgogi* (horse meat) was forbidden during that time in order to protect the horse population.

At Majodan ("Horse Ancestor Altar"), located near today's KAL Hotel intersection in Jeju City, rituals were historically held to pray for the horses' fecundity. A monument marks the original site atop a picturesque hill.

"Horse drivers" are experts trained in traditional animal husbandry

techniques to raise and live in close proximity with horses. A children's book called *Majimak Taeuri (The Last Horse Driver)*, written by Bak Jae-hyeong of the Jeju Office of Education, tells the story of 82-year-old Go Tae-u, who has spent his entire life with horses.

"In the old days," Go recalls, "every family raised horses, so we took turns rounding them up and taking them to graze in the mountains, where the grass was good. Horse drivers were the professionals who did this, while everyone else simply looked after the horses when their turn came." His call to the horses is like a spiritual melody that allows him to communicate with these animals.

Horses on Jeju can graze in the spring, summer, and autumn without supplementary feeding, but require feeding in winter (top).

The *teuri kosa* is a rite that takes place on the 15th day of the lunar month of July on Jeju Island. The *teuri* ("cowherds" in the Jeju dialect) who raise horses and cows go to the pastures and pray for the health and safety of their animals (bottom).

After the advent of the automobile, horses lost their traditional function. In 1984, fewer than 1,000 purebred horses lived on Jeju Island, and in 1986 a few dozen horses of proper pedigree were designated as natural monuments.

Today, figures from the provincial government put the local horse population at 1,392 Jeju horses (200 of them purebreds with registered pedigree), 4,179 thoroughbreds, and 16,692 hybrid Halla horses, for a total of 22,223. These are raised by 1,157 farm households around the island, and 1,000 are slaughtered every year for consumption. Horse-racing is a popular Jeju sport.

Jeju's unique horses can be seen in fields throughout the island, especially in the foothills of Mt. Halla as one drives between Jeju City and Seogwipo along 5.16 Road. Many places provide horseback riding to the public: in the Halla foothills, in the countryside, and along the coast.

Jeju's Ecological Future

Jeju's ecosystem is extraordinarily well preserved. But modernization and the island's dependency on tourism, as well as the development of large projects deemed critical for Jeju's economic future, have recently been prompting concerns.

The struggle between ecological preservation and economic development is common among societies around the world. Jeju, in recognition of its natural assets and remembrance of its close historical relationship—kinship, even—with its environment, is taking many steps to strike a careful balance. Environmental education, including eco-tours and cultural tourism, is a focus of the island's development. One example of this preservation can be found in endeavors like the government-sponsored "Gotjawal Trust."

With UNESCO status comes responsibility: the need for

Members of several environmental groups work to restore the habitat of *sambaekcho* (*Saururus chinensis*; sometimes known as Chinese lizardtail), an endangered species.

education, careful eco-tourism, and environmental preservation in order to maintain such designations. Acquiring this recognition helps to preserve Jeju's natural heritage.

Jeju will also host the World Conservation Congress of the International Union for the Conservation of Nature (IUCN) in 2012. In preparation for this event, the island's international convention center is undergoing a massive renovation according to "green," or environmentally sound, construction principles. A Jeju Nature School has recently been established for children, and an international effort is under way to develop a World Environment University on the island.

Additionally, experimentation with other ecologically beneficial practices is taking place on Jeju. At a Smart-Grid Testbed, research is currently being conducted in a number of related categories. There are also land-and sea-based wind farms for efficiency studies and, on outlying Gapado, a particularly ambitious long-term project through which the island's inhabitants and researchers hope to convert the

island to completely carbon emission-free status within 25 years. Nine farms on the tiny island have also eliminated the use of pesticides in a government-sponsored program for eco-friendly agriculture.

Jeju is determined to preserve its nature in the face of the challenges brought by modernization.

The *Seonjakjiwat* Korean fir forest, located at 1,650m above sea level (top), and the Yeongsil pine forest, located at 1,250m above sea level (bottom), have been chosen as sample areas by the Mt. Halla ecosystem department of a local environmental resource research institute for prediction and analysis of the effects of climate change on Mt. Halla's ecosystem and development of an adaptation strategy.

Oreum: A Special Relationship

Oreum is the local word for the small mountains or peaks that arose to dot the island from beneath the earth following the eruptions of Mt. Halla. Officially, they are "secondary," "lateral," "satellite," or "parasitic" volcanic cones of various types, including cinder and scoria cones, tuff cones and rings, and lava domes. There are 368 of them on Jeju, ranging in height from 100 to 700 meters.

"You can hike one each day of the year and have three left over," a common saying among Jeju residents goes. Many express a kinship with these structures, and there are more in this cluster around a central volcano than at

any other location in the world. They, along with Mt. Halla, serve to define the topography of the island.

The word *oreum*, suffixed to a cone's name, is replaced by *bong* when the peak is at sea (e.g., Ilchulbong or Sarabong) and *san* to indicate a mountain (e.g., Hallasan or Sanbangsan)—although the distinction in the latter case is rather vague. The people of Jeju hike the *oreum* regularly, building shamanic shrines, temples, the conical stacked stone prayer structures known as *bangsatap*, and exercise equipment on a majority of them. Most of the *oreum* have craters, which are referred to locally as *gumburi* and, like many extraordinary features of nature on Jeju, are associated with the divine.

Each *oreum* has a name, many of them descriptive. One example is the

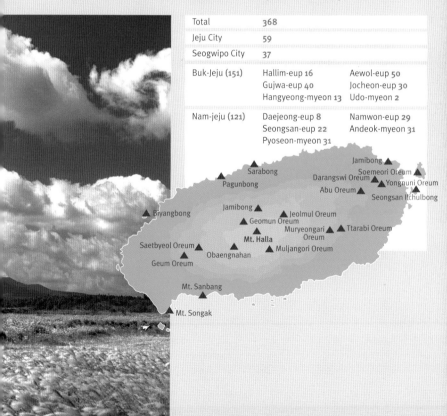

Total	368	
Jeju City	59	
Seogwipo City	37	
Buk-Jeju (151)	Hallim-eup 16	Aewol-eup 50
	Gujwa-eup 40	Jocheon-eup 30
	Hangyeong-myeon 13	Udo-myeon 2
Nam-jeju (121)	Daejeong-eup 8	Namwon-eup 29
	Seongsan-eup 22	Andeok-myeon 31
	Pyoseon-myeon 31	

famous, UNESCO-designated Seongsan Ilchulbong. With both *san* and *bong suffixes*, it translates into English as "Castle Mountain, Sunrise Peak" and is a tuff cone with a wide crater from which one can watch the sunrise across the sea. Every New Year's Eve, there is a festival at this site, with thousands spending the frigid night atop the cone to observe the first seaside sunrise of the new year.

Another beloved *oreum* is nearby Yongnuni. With a name meaning "dragon's eye," this *oreum is said to look like* a dragon lying on its side. It was the favorite site of renowned photographer Kim Young Gap, who believed it to be one of the most beautiful settings on Jeju. He particularly loved how different it looked from every angle.

Sarabong, a seaside *oreum* located in Jeju City, provides a natural escape from the urban life below. It is the home of the Chilmeori *dang*, or shamanic shrine, where the annual Yeongdeung *gut*, or ritual, for the Goddess of Wind and Sea is held. It is also home to the Mochung Buddhist temple, on the grounds of which Kim Man-deok, Jeju's most historic female icon, is buried and a small memorial hall is kept in her name. The *oreum* is famous for its view of the sunset over the water, which has earned its own special term: *sabong nakjo*.

Abu Oreum is another beloved peak, which is often photographed in the different seasons. It has a semicircle of evergreen trees in the middle of its crater and a population of horses. Suwolbong and Yongmeori Oreum, both seaside tuff rings similar to Seongsan Ilchulbong, are also favorites for their stunning beauty;

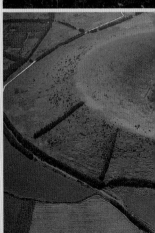

Yongmeori, or "dragon's head," is especially remarkable for its unusual seaside cliffs and was designated as one of the island's Geopark sites.

Mt. Sanbang is a giant lava dome and the oldest rock formation on Jeju Island. This bell-shaped mountain is also a Geopark site and can be seen from nearly every part of Jeju. It matches the size and shape of the crater on Mt. Halla; an ancient legend tells of an angry god who, in a fit of rage, plucked off the top of Halla and threw it to the southwest of the island, where it became Mt. Sanbang.

Geomun Oreum, a UNESCO-designated World Natural Heritage and Geopark site, is a unique structure of nine caves and a system of lava tubes, including Manjang Cave, which has the longest such tube in the world. "Geomun" has two meanings in Jeju dialect: "black" and "divine." It bears an exceptionally large crater with nine peaks and a smaller cone in the center, called an Aroreum. It is referred to by locals as "the nine dragons playing with a Chintamani stone," referring to a wish-granting stone of ancient India's Hindu and Buddhist traditions, often depicted throughout Asia in the mouth of a dragon. Geomun Oreum also houses a 35m vertical lava tube, a gorge that gives the appearance of a valley, and a microclimate all its own. One of the four *gotjawal* rainforests occupies the same area as Geomun Oreum, which is a very complex *oreum* indeed.

To Jeju people, the *oreum* are members of their family. To visitors, they provide endless opportunities to experience Jeju's nature in a direct and personal way.

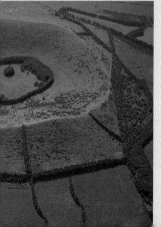

Chapter Three

ISLAND OF WOMEN

Beyond the gently waving fields of bright yellow rape flowers heaves the deep blue ocean. With only gourds for support, *haenyeo* (women divers), ranging in age from young to very old, freely plumb the ocean's depths. They are heroines who hold the sea deep in their hearts. Both their life and their death are found in that ocean. "When we measure the depth of the ocean and dive down one or two body lengths, we pass between life and death," one of them says. Today, they are the living goddesses of Jeju Island.

The myths and shamanist songs of Jeju often feature female protagonists. They serve as a medium bringing Jeju and the outside world together. They also give their bodies over to creation, while unreservedly carving out independent lives. With a strong sense of self-awareness and adventure, the women of Jeju see no need to act cautious or bashful in front of men; they choose their own husbands, and draw upon their courage, wisdom, and ability in reacting swiftly to save their communities from danger.

JEJU WOMEN: WHO THEY ARE

The lives of all people are unquestionably shaped to a great extent by their environment. And while the women of Jeju Island are born of the same seed as other Koreans, there is no denying that they possess certain very distinctive characteristics due to Jeju's island nature.

Since the dawn of Jeju civilization, life on the island has been influenced by its women, and in particular by their capacity for action and aggressive instinct. The life journey of the island's women has always been considered singular and unique.

From the typical spatial perspective, an island is a small and restricted piece of land. Seen from another perspective, however, an island is an infinite space where the sky and sea come together.

Jeju Island is a place where open space is as broad as the heavens

The women of Jeju Island are strong, independent, and assertive. The female divers are representative of these Jeju women. Jeju's women divers collect shellfish from the waters off the island without any diving apparatus, wearing only simple swimsuits, flippers, and masks.

Surrounded by sky and water, the island is both limited and limitlessly expanding.
It is the natural environment of Jeju that created its tenacious women.

and as deep as the sea, where the seasons come and go in a regular pattern and time moves as it should. Though the land may seem to stop at the water's edge, beneath the sea it stretches into infinity. It is these geographic and topographic conditions that have exerted such an unmistakable influence on the disposition of the people who have made this island their home.

Traditionally, the women of Jeju Island have been described as gregarious in temperament, open and artless, strong-willed and unbound by the constraints of the "feminine." They are seen as self-motivated and steadfast in the way they tackle what life deals them, courageous and pioneering in spirit, content despite the long hard hours of labor they must put in to survive, industrious and resilient in the face of the harshest of conditions, and warmhearted, with a generous willingness to help others. As mentioned before, these characteristics of the female islanders are rooted in the fact that Jeju is an island.

Specific conditions related to Jeju Island's geographic characteristics include isolation from the mainland, the dryness of the land and scarcity of water, and the strong, relentless buffeting of wind. In the present as in the past, it is necessary to adapt to these natural conditions and, at times, to exploit them. Indeed, life on Jeju Island is rewarding in its own way.

Although the practice is limited today to a handful of seaside

Gods and rituals are part of everyday life for the women of Jeju, who must spend their lives on the boundary of life and death in the water.

villages, people from the distant past until today have been able to earn a livelihood by diving and drawing on the diverse resources offered by the sea. The fruits of the sea thus collected add to the richness of life by providing diversity and contributing to household earnings. These conditions have served to ensure little disparity between rich and poor; all were able to live in equality, and all were

The women of Jeju live lives of enjoyment and independence, neither shying away from a difficult and treacherous livelihood nor resenting their lot.

Yeongdeung Gut

Between February and mid-March, the windswept island of Jeju is often gripped by a fickle cold. This time is known there as "Yeongdeung Month," marking the visit of Grandmother Yeongdeung, the goddess of the wind. At this time, it is customary for residents to suspend all regular activities: fishing at sea (including the women divers who gather shellfish from the ocean floor), moving, repairing homes, traveling, and even wallpapering.

To the Jeju residents, who make their living from the sea, the wind is an element that controls their lives and livelihoods. For this reason, shamanic rituals are regularly held at seaside villages to pray for safety and abundance. The Yeongdeung *gut* (ritual) at Chilmeori *dang* (shrine), or *Chilmeori-dang Yeongdeung-gut*, is a representative ritual for promoting the community's well-being. It was designated an Important Intangible Cultural Property by the South Korean government in 1980, and an Intangible Cultural Heritage of Humanity by UNESCO in 2009.

The ritual consists of three separate parts: welcome and farewell rites held two weeks apart, and an additional rite held on Soseom (Udo), or "Cow Island," where Grandmother Yeongdeung is said to stay over for one day before returning home.

Wearing a scarlet robe and a black hat with a peacock feather in it, *Keun-*

simbang—Great Shaman Kim Yun-su—began this year's rite by dancing and telling a story. Twenty-two men and women from the Yeongdeung Rites Preservation Society, including Kim's wife, *simbang* Lee Yong-ok, provided the musical accompaniment. Also present were several hereditary *simbang* from longtime *simbang* families.

"The rite begins with the opening of the storage chest that holds the spirit tablets of the deities," says Kim. "After all, it is only when the lid is opened that the deities can come out to take part. There is a dance for the opening of the lid, and a dance for checking inside the chest. First, I invite the deities to attend the ritual, and then I check to make sure that no deities are left behind. I then help to seat them. I recite the history of the rite and entertain the guest of honor, Grandmother Yeongdeung, to the best of my ability with the food offerings and with song and dance. Then I ask for a bountiful catch and pray that she will take away all misfortune when she leaves." He adds, "It is a ceremony not unlike those held when receiving important guests of the state today. We even engage in negotiations [between shaman and deity], discussing what to give and what to take."

Lee notes, "We know that the gods are watching us from all around, so we concentrate and bow to them with all courtesy, and at those times we feel their weight resting on our shoulders." These days, the number of rituals held on Jeju has decreased dramatically. "Before, the fishing boat owners were all Jeju locals, and there were more *haenyeo* [diving women] as well, so we had many more tables for the food offerings," Lee says. "But now, there are fewer *haenyeo*, and the fishing boat owners are mainlanders. Still, now that this ritual has been designated a cultural heritage, people seem to find it quite comforting. I intend to do everything in my power to see that it is preserved." The public is invited to the *gut*, with written guides and other materials provided in English as well as Korean. Enter from the west side of Sarabong near the docks, pass the lighthouse, and you will soon arrive at the Chilmeori *dang* area.

Jeju's Yeongdeung *gut* (also called the Chilmeori *dang gut*) (left)
Keun-simbang, the Great Shaman Kim Yun-su (right)

guaranteed a certain degree of material comfort. In addition, the psychological stress of living in isolation was minimal with the mainland out of sight; indeed, this actually helped in instilling a positive outlook toward life on the island.

Groups of female professional divers sharing the same workplace have been present in seaside villages for nearly two millennia. With their special and unique characteristics, these communities of divers exert a distinct influence

1. The *bulteok* is where the diving women change clothes, future divers are trained, and the women engage in discussions to establish their community. The word "*bulteok*" refers to a stone bonfire ring on the beach where the Jeju women divers congregate for their diving.
2. Recreation of a *bulteok* at Jeju's Haenyeo Museum

| 1 | 2 |

Jeju's women divers do not dive alone except under special circumstances. Because of the dangers of their sea labor, they must work together to help out when one is in danger, and the rules of the community are based in an equitable distribution of income, with all divers working at the same time and place under the same conditions, each earning what she can.
1. Women divers in the early 20th century. Their outfits were thinner than the ones worn today.
2. Modern Jeju women divers at work

on the life of the islanders. The societies first formed near natural outdoor formations called *bulteok*, which the women divers used for changing clothes. It was here that the women reared their children and taught them to dive. With their own ways of work, worship, and leisure, the women divers eventually came to forge a unique lifestyle, one that has become part of the rich culture of Jeju Island.

SONGS OF THE DIVING WOMEN

Jeju has a strong tradition of collective labor accompanied by song. Two distinctive characteristics of this music are the alternation of corresponding phrases between a lead singer and the chorus and, in the farming songs, a freestyle rhythm thought to stem from a lack of musical instruments on the island until recently. The a capella aspect also provides a vocal ornamentation characteristic of plainsong. Threshing and rowing songs, on the other hand, contained contrasting short and simple phrases repeated with matching body movements.

Jeju people were known to be gifted in rhythm. In one charming custom, groups of women returning from the well with pottery water jars known as *heobeok* would stop to rest, set the jars in front of them, and begin beating on them with their hands to create a drumming sound, to which they would improvise a song.

The women of Jeju created pleasure in an exhausting routine by singing and dancing together by the water with their *heobeok* (water jars) before them.

Jeju's Haenyeo Museum features a traditional diving culture performance on Saturdays by Kim Young-ja and Kang Deung-ja, holders of Intangible Cultural Heritage No. 1, the *haenyeo* songs.

The diving women had their own songs, typically sung as they rowed to and from their diving sites. The "Song of the *Haenyeo*," sung throughout the majority of Jeju's villages, included lyrics such as "This small woman's mind shakes with the grief of a lifetime;", "Merciful Dragon Sea God / Although we have good fortune / With abalone and conchs galore / Please let me dive in peace;" and "My youth is all spent / . . . / The child becomes white-haired soon enough." Interspersed with these words were haunting repetitions of the refrain "Ieodo, Ieodo," referring to a mythical next world.

Other songs of the diving women include those sung by the *chulga haenyeo*, referring to those working away from home on the mainland or abroad. There were songs of the Japanese resistance movement, "merrymaking" songs intended purely for pleasure, and many more. The songs served to lighten the burden of their hard work, loneliness, and sorrow.

Today, these songs are kept by officially designated skills holders. Kim Young-ja and Kang Deung-ja are two individuals who possess the *haenyeo* songs, carrying them on for future generations. These two women have been performing the songs every Saturday afternoon at the Haenyeo Museum in Hado Village, on the eastern shore of Jeju, since April 2011. Initially scheduled to last for one month, their performance has been so wildly popular that it has been extended several times. They are accompanied by four musicians playing traditional instruments, along with a dozen or so dancers and performers, all members of the Sara Art Company. Audience members are encouraged to participate in singing, dancing, and *heobeok* drumming.

THE TWO AXES OF FEMALE SOCIETY ON JEJU ISLAND

More than half of all the islands scattered throughout the world are inhabited by humans. Life on many islands is the same in that it has been led from the beginning by hardy and resilient women. The Jeju divers, who are representative of a naturally occurring women's culture in an ordinary male-female cooperative society, provide a rare example of a community group that has been carried on for generations.

An inland thatched-roof home (left) and a thatched-roof home on the shore (right)

The divers, however, are not the only women who have forged their own unique culture on Jeju Island. The women who live in hillside villages and high atop mountains have contributed just as much as the women of the coast to creating Jeju's special way of life. As such, the pattern of life that can be found on the mid-slope areas of Mt. Halla is just as special as that found along the coast.

In the past, there were two major spheres of influence on Jeju Island: the diving communities of the coastal areas and the farming communities of the mid-slope areas. Though both were female-oriented communities, they maintained different ways of behavior and thought. The farming islanders' way of thinking was largely influenced by the island's use as a place of exile by Joseon Dynasty (1392-1910) rulers who subscribed to Confucianism. Over time, the islanders began to adopt the ways of the exiles. There was a government office in the mid-slope villages, and it was in the nearby communities that most of the exiles lived. It was thus natural that the farmers of the mid-slope regions would become familiar with Confucian customs. In terms of the work ethic, there was no reason for the farming villages to forge a different way of life from the diving villages. But the women of the farming villages were as steeped in Confucian ways as those of the mainland. The women of the rural communities sought to differentiate themselves from the divers, who stripped to near nudity before diving into the sea and were therefore considered a lowly segment.

The divers, however, were not concerned with whether the farmers looked down on them. They considered the rural women rigid and stuck in their ways, as well as ignorant of real freedom in life. Both groups had little desire to interact socially. As a result,

The clothing worn by the women in their daily life covered their arms and legs (left), whereas their diving uniforms exposed their shoulders and legs (right). From a Confucian standpoint, these uniforms were tantamount to public nudity.

while the two groups traded goods, they engaged in few other forms of exchange. They avoided intermarriage between communities and maintained a considerable degree of exclusivity from one another.

The barriers between the two groups of women have now been broken down for the most part, and the essential qualities of Jeju women have all been diluted over time. This is the result of major changes in the island's living conditions. The divers still exist today, but not in the same form as before.

TRACING THE ORIGINS OF JEJU'S WOMEN

The origins of the lives of Jeju women are well preserved in many legends that remain extant today. The first Jeju woman was a goddess known as Grandmother Seolmundae, who created the island. The title "grandmother" can be interpreted in two ways: the word has its literal sense, but it is also used as a highly honorific title for a woman, much like "elder." In this case, the latter meaning applies. Unlike other gods of creation, Seolmundae had no absolute authority or power, but her every act bears a trace of the intimate mother of Jeju Island. In essence, Seolmundae is akin to the goddesses of Greece and Rome, and especially the goddess of the earth, Gaia or Terra. Her creation of Jeju Island was near perfection, with no ecological flaws. But there was once a time when Jeju Island was considered unfit for human habitation. Because of its extreme wind, drought, and flooding, it was called the island of "the three disasters." There were times when severe drought caused terrible suffering, but there were no prolonged dry periods. Rain eventually came to douse the earth, sometimes bringing floods. Psychologically, however, there was the understanding that water was there on the island, if only from a temporary natural phenomenon. These days, when it is no longer possible to rely only on surface and spring water, Jeju Island makes use of its plentiful supply of underground water. Seolmundae's capability, wisdom, and care in creating the island as an adaptable land whose environment and conditions could be regulated for survival purposes are only now more fully understood.

Grandmother Seolmundae by Jeju woodblock artist Hong Jin-suk (top) A Grandmother Seolmundae Festival with a ceremony to honor the goddess (bottom)

Numerous models for the typical Jeju woman can be found in the myth of Seolmundae. According to lore, Seolmundae made Jeju Island with her own hands, carrying earth to and from it in the folds of her skirt. This shows a capacity for hard work that would be passed on to posterity. The myth also says that she worked laboriously until her only skirt became so tattered that it was unfit to wear. This symbolized the fact that life on the island was not abundant in material terms. Seolmundae wished for a pair of drawers that would cover her legs, allowing her to continue her work and connect Jeju Island to the mainland. In the intensity of her efforts, we can spy the special characteristics of Jeju women, who do not despair under even the harshest conditions, their pioneering spirit and strong will enabling them to take on any challenge.

Seolmundae was also Jeju Island's first diver. According to a version of the story that is told in the Pyoseon Village region, Seolmundae first dived into the sea to gather food when she was pregnant with her five hundred sons, who were called the "five hundred

The five hundred sons of Grandmother Seolmundae became the Yeongsil Rocks of Mt. Halla.

generals." The story has been passed down over the years mixed with bawdy tales describing her movements in the water. The myth ends with Seolmundae throwing herself into a pot of gruel to provide food for her sons. The storyline here should be interpreted from the perspective of feminism, in that it describes the womanly attribute of helping others and the spirit of self-sacrifice seen among Jeju's women.

In addition to Seolmundae, other goddesses such as Segyeong, the earth mother, and Jacheongbi, the goddess of agriculture, provide models for the women of Jeju, who have enjoyed equal standing with men and lived full, active lives. If we take a closer look at these myths, we can easily imagine how Jeju women lived in the past. For example, Jacheongbi went out to do the laundry on her fifteenth birthday and never returned home. This was a sign that she had reached adulthood and ventured out into the world on her own. She proposed marriage to a man she met at the washing place, and they went to Okhwang to study. This story reveals the place of women in traditional Jeju society: receiving the protection of their parents in their youth and becoming their own people, free to act without restrictions, upon reaching adulthood. The initiative Jacheongbi showed in proposing marriage to a man is something that was, until very recently, unthinkable in Korean society. This provides evidence that the act of proposing marriage was not restricted to one particular sex in traditional mainland Jeju society. It is said that Jacheongbi received from her father-in-law the present of seeds for five grains. By planting them on the island, she laid the groundwork for the belief that the island's agricultural society was initiated and led by women. The myth also indicates that Jeju women were on an equal footing with men and emphasizes the concept that there was no inherent difference between men and women in terms of their appearance or their activities and work.

In general, female societies are said to be weaker than male ones in various aspects. But numerous examples exist to show that the female society of Jeju Island was exceptional in many ways. One example involves the intense battle that the women divers waged against the Japanese colonial authorities. In the history of Korea's movement to gain independence from Japanese colonialism, this

The Anti-Japanese Struggle of the Haenyeo by Kang Yo-bae, 1989

stands out as the only example of a women's professional group taking collective action. Though their anti-Japanese activities may be seen as a fight to protect their own ability to survive, the fact that it was organized and sustained in the first place is meaningful in both historical and social terms.

After Korea's liberation from Japanese colonial rule, the women divers continued as a group in making efforts for the community's well-being. For example, they would designate certain diving grounds from which all proceeds would be donated to educational authorities for the establishment of schools in seaside villages where there were none. Even today, there is an offshore area that is known as the "school sea." And even in the turmoil of the April 3rd Uprising, many Jeju women sacrificed themselves to save others.

When all is said and done, it was the Jeju women's capacity for work that enabled them to sustain their regional societies and economies. There is no question that they have been the island's driving economic force. The Jeju women established a system of

Elderly women who took part in the 1932 uprising of women divers against the Japanese

production based on a division of labor that survives to this day.

The women of Jeju Island are still highly active in the island's economy. According to statistics, Jeju Island has the highest percentage of women in the workforce in Korea. About 58 percent of women over the age of 15 are economically active.

WOMEN OF MODESTY AND CHARITY

In the past, every Jeju homemaker had a special crock where she would store food in preparation for the future. At each meal, she would place a handful of uncooked rice in the crock. The woman of the house had complete authority over this crock, and it can be said that this kind of frugality laid the foundation for the prosperity Jeju Island enjoys today.

On Jeju Island, it was customary for married children to leave the family home and set up their own households. The idea behind this was to maintain small households that were compact and economically sound, with autonomy in domestic matters.

Today, it has become increasingly difficult to maintain the traditional ways of the Jeju woman because the basic environment

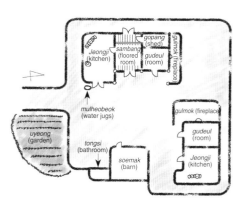

Floor plan for a Jeju home. Daughters generally left home, after marrying, but even when they lived together with their family they lived independently with separate kitchens.

has changed so drastically. Still, the basis of island life has not really changed in essence: the women of Jeju Island have as much influence on the shaping of life today as in the past.

The community-based way of life that is another striking characteristic of Jeju Island's female society still has significant influence; despite today's individualistic lifestyles, the islanders still hold on to the values of mutual dependence and assistance between neighbors.

In general, when people reach the stage of self-support, self-sufficiency and independence, they become less conscious of how other people may judge them. They become freer, and their reliance on others lessens. Life on Jeju Island has always been this way, and Jeju women have always embodied this philosophy.

Though it is possible to skim the surface of the subject of Jeju women, to talk about who they are and how they live, it is difficult to really pin them down in any way. But there is a great pleasure that comes from simply accepting Jeju women as they are.

KIM MAN-DEOK

Like the island goddesses, the women of Jeju possess a sense of self-identity and inner strength that allows them to blaze their own trails in life. As they struggled to satisfy the demands of the royal court amid the barren natural environment of Jeju, the women of long ago had to perform like superhuman beings.

Jeju's first known female merchant, Kim Man-deok (1739-1812), not only lived an independent life but was charitable as well. She lost her parents at the age of 12 and was forced to make her own way in life. She fought to rise above her station as a *gisaeng* (entertainer and courtesan) by developing a head for business. She did not succumb to her adverse circumstances, and she eventually succeeded in trade as the first female merchant and entrepreneur in Korea, which enabled her to amass a personal fortune and demonstrate a sense of community-mindedness.

Standard funeral portrait of Kim Man-deok

The people of Jeju grow up hearing that they "owe everything to Grandmother Man-deok." When a severe famine swept the island in 1794, Kim used her entire fortune to buy rice, saving 1,100 residents of Jeju from starvation. When King Jeongjo learned of her generous deed, he told her he would grant her anything she desired. Kim told the king that she wanted to visit Mt. Geumgang (Diamond Mountain). She thus became the first resident of Jeju to travel to the mainland and visit this sacred mountain, thereby ending a two-century prohibition against travel that had denied the people of Jeju the option of visiting the peninsula.

The Kim Man-deok Festival is held every year in early October to honor the woman who rescued Jeju's islanders from famine.

This prohibition dated back to the early Joseon era, when the men of Jeju took to the sea to fulfill the heavy burden of military service and provide local tribute to the royal court. They suffered greatly when they were mobilized to maintain the island's defensive fortifications and deliver tributary items such as mandarin oranges, horses, and abalone. Over time, a growing number of residents relocated to the mainland to escape this burden. This led the royal court to impose a 1629 prohibition preventing island people from visiting the mainland, and to mobilize women as well for military duty. For this reason, the gathering of abalone, which had previously been done by men, became the work of women from the 17th century onward. The diving women had to supply the abalone they gathered as tribute to the royal court or as tax payments to the local government.

As a result, the sea became everything to the women of Jeju, their means of survival and everyday life. They began diving as children and continued to reap the sea's bounty as they became elderly veterans with exceptional diving abilities. At times, they would put their lives at risk, diving into the treacherous depths to earn their livelihood. Even when they gave birth, they would return to the water after only a three-day rest.

In 1977, Kim Man-deok's grave was moved from its original site in Hwabuk-dong to its current place on the grounds of Mochung Temple, located on the east side of Sarabong in Jeju City. It is a place of pilgrimage for many Korean women. A small memorial hall in her honor is maintained there by the monks.

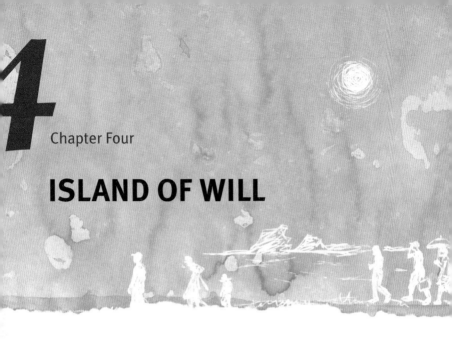

Chapter Four

ISLAND OF WILL

Jeju's people are known to be stalwart, tenacious, frugal, independent of spirit, free-thinking, and strong-willed, as well as outspoken and simultaneously welcoming and suspicious of outsiders. With what has been referred to as the "Tamna mindset," the island has made the transition from functioning independently—first as a tribal agrarian society, and then an independent regency trading with and influenced by its neighbors—to experiencing a series of invasions and resistance efforts, along with occupation and subjugation by others.

Furthermore, for the 5,000 years that they have lived on this island, the people of Jeju have had to struggle merely to subsist under harsh natural topographic and climatic elements. As a result, they formed multiple collective labor practices, economic cooperatives, systems of village-oriented kinship, and a myriad of other practices of mutual aid.

Jeju's history of hardship and sorrow has resulted in the collective psychological strength and community bond characteristic of this island society.

A HISTORY OF MISFORTUNE, BANISHMENT, AND SUFFERING

Jeju Island is known for its "three abundances," or *samda*: rocks, wind, and women. In contrast, ancient Jeju locals spoke of excessive rocks, wind, and drought. In other words, *samda* for the islanders did not represent a sentimental empathy for natural phenomena, but natural obstacles that posed a challenge to their very existence. The history of the volcanic island of Jeju is the history of everyday lives for a steadfast, resolute people forced to cultivate barren fields and endure incessant wind and droughts.

The island was first settled over 10,000 years ago. Evidence of the first inhabitants of the island can be found at a prehistoric site in Gosan Village in Hangyong Township. Home to the oldest relics on the island, the Gosan site is very significant in understanding the origin of the Jeju people. Excavations of the site have yielded an abundance of pottery shards and stone tools, including exquisitely fashioned arrowheads.

The characteristics of Jeju's people are their diligence, thrift, strong will, positive and cheerful personality, and spirit of cooperation.

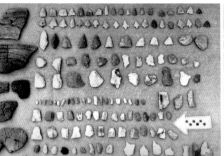

Prehistory earthenware and stoneware relics excavated from Gosan Village (left)
Prehistoric site in Samyang Village (right)

The area's ancient inhabitants used the arrowheads to hunt and apparently caught fish along the nearby coast and in the marshes. The primitive pottery unearthed suggests that in addition to hunting and fishing, the people also experimented with agriculture.

Scattered along coastal areas, the inhabitants gradually organized themselves into community groups. The legend of the "three clans" attests to this process. The ancient story describes how clans—represented in the legend by three divine figures known as Ko, Yang, and Bu—transformed the island into a state known as Tamna.

In the legend, these three demigods came out of a hole in the ground at Moheunghyeol (now Samseonghyeol) and took up residence in the area. One day, they discovered a giant wooden box that had washed up on a beach on the east coast. Inside the box, they found the seeds for five grains, a horse, a cow, and three princesses from a country called Byeongnang. The three divine figures married these princesses and began to expand their influence on the island. They engaged in agriculture and raised livestock. Eventually, they were able to create the kingdom called Tamna.

In ancient records, Tamna is known by a number of different names, including Takna, Somna, Tammora, and Chuho. It should be kept in mind that ancient Tamna was not the dominion of any other state on the Korean peninsula, but an independent kingdom that enjoyed reciprocal trade ties and diplomatic exchanges with China, Japan, and the states on the Korean Peninsula. Rather than being an isolated island in the middle of the ocean, it was a strategic base for maritime exchange within Northeast Asia.

Around the latter part of the third century, according to the Chinese work *Samguozhi (History of the Three Kingdoms)*, Tamna was already conducting trade with the three Han states in the southern part of the Korean Peninsula. Chinese currency dating to around the first century was discovered in Sanji Harbor in 1928, providing further proof that ancient Tamna engaged in active maritime trade. From the late fifth to tenth centuries, Tamna expanded its commercial activities to Goguryeo, Unified Silla, Tang China, and Japan.

"Samseonghyeol" refers to the three holes where the progenitors of the island's Ko, Yang, and Bu clans are said to have emerged. Legend has it that these divine figures dressed in leather and hunted for food before marrying the three princesses of Byeongnang—who brought with them the five grains, a horse, and a cow—and beginning lives of agriculture.

STONE CULTURE

The unique features of Jeju Island are often summed up as the *samda*, or "three abundances": rocks, wind, and women. The *samda* are generally regarded as negative features, but the islanders have adroitly turned them to their advantage. In particular, they have creatively capitalized on perhaps the most difficult of the three: the area's numerous rocks.

Geumneung Stone Garden

Bangsatap

On Jeju, rocks have long been used to build walls around crop fields and grave sites, as well as fortresses, breakwaters, buildings, and tutelary pagodas. They have even been used for carving *dolharubang* ("stone grandfather") figures, which once served as symbolic sentry figures outside of gates but are now primarily sold as souvenirs. In these ways, the island's ubiquitous rocks have become an essential aspect of its lifestyle and culture.

In addition to functioning as boundaries, the stone walls around fields served as barriers against another of the island's abundances: wind. The stone walls have irregular surfaces filled with holes. But a closer look at their construction reveals the builder's exquisite skill. Large stones are stacked and the cracks are filled with small pebbles, but holes are created in the walls at regular intervals. At first glance, this makes the walls appear very precarious. Yet by letting air through, the holes actually keep the structures from being toppled by strong gusts.

A number of dome-shaped stone pagodas, called *bangsatap*, can be found at tourist sites such as Mokseokwon Garden and Sangumburi. These are the tutelary pagodas, derived from the Joseon era pagoda placed near villages to ward off evil. According to principles of geomancy, these pagodas were set up in "empty" spots as symbolic bulwarks against negative forces. It is said that before such pagodas came into being, a broken cauldron or some other similar object was placed on the ground. Even now, the original form of these pagodas can be seen at Iho-dong in Jeju City and various other places around the island.

In addition to using stones for walls around fields, the islanders stacked them to create "sea fields." At various points along the coast, villagers used stones to block off part of the shore and create small basins called *wondam*—similar to the manmade fish ponds found on the islands of Hawaii. Typically, individuals or villages would manage a few of these basin areas, while some villages had as many as five or six of them. The *wondam* would trap anchovies, octopuses, eel, and other fish that came in with the tide and were unable to get back out as the tide ebbed. Whenever there was a large catch, there would be a great feast on the coast. Folk songs sung during this time, such as the "Song of the Anchovy Harvest," have been passed down to the present day.

In addition to being utilized for the living, stones were used to provide structures for the dead. Tombs from this region, called *yongmyo* (dragon graves), have a distinctive design, typically surrounded by a double wall of stacked stone. In addition to walls, graves included statues of children or mother sculptures. The expressions and poses of the child figures differ noticeably among the regions of the island, providing important clues to everyday life and thinking among the villagers during various eras.

These are good examples of the infinite potential of human wisdom and determination to overcome difficult circumstances. The Jeju people's ingenious use of stone can be seen everywhere throughout the island.

Ruins of a Jeju castle built in the Tamna era and used in the Goryeo era to defend against Japanese raiders (top)
Yongmyo (stone-ringed Jeju tombs) (bottom)

East Asia in the seventh century. The independent Tamna, the precursor of Jeju Island, was not an isolated place but a key maritime trade center for the region.

In particular, the fall of Baekje in 660 allowed the island to engage in independent diplomacy free from Baekje interference. From the fifth lunar month in 661 to the second lunar month in 662, Tamna sent envoys to Silla, Tang China, and Japan and made considerable efforts to monitor the international political environment. In 661 and 665, the Tamna king and envoys visited the Tang royal palace. During the "rites to heaven" held at Taishan Mountain, they participated as equals with representatives from Silla, Baekje, and Japan—an indication that Tang China accorded Tamna the same diplomatic respect it extended to other nations in the region. Tamna was also actively involved in events on the peninsula. During the 663 Baek River Battle, part of an effort to revive the Baekje Kingdom, Tamna supported Baekje and Japanese forces.

In a development related to this external exchange, the political and social ruling class responsible for diplomacy and trade flourished as Tamna grew into a strong state. Around the seventh century, Silla's Queen Seondeok erected a massive nine-story pagoda at Hwangnyong Temple in the Silla capital, today's Gyeongju, as a spiritual bulwark to fend off invasions from nine countries. It is interesting to note that Tamna was fourth on the list of countries. Ancient Tamna's status as a maritime state can also be surmised from the fact that around the eighth and ninth centuries. Tang China regarded it as an important trading partner.

With the rise of the Goryeo Dynasty during the 10th century, Tamna soon lost its standing as an independent state. As Goryeo power came to extend as far south as Tamna, the island kingdom finally became a territory of its mainland counterpart in 1105. During the reign of Goryeo's King Gojong (1213–1259), Tamna's name was changed to "Jeju," which generally meant "province across the sea."

ANTI-MONGOLIAN RESISTANCE AND SUBJUGATION

In the immediate wake of the annexation, the islanders suffered greatly from the burden of having to offer tribute to the Goryeo regency. On a number of occasions, the islanders rebelled against the exploitative demands of the government. When the Three Elite Patrols (Sambyeolcho), a military troop from the mainland that had worked its way down from Ganghwa Island to Jeju, revolted against the central government and the occupying Mongols on the island in 1270, the islanders joined forces with them. As the island residents mobilized for the struggle, they built a number of fortifications such as the Hangpaduri, Aewolmok, and Hwanhaejang fortresses, which were built along the coast to prevent enemy landings. Their remains can still be seen in the villages of Goseong, Gonae, and Aewol.

After the subjugation of the Three Elite Patrols, Jeju Island came under the direct control of the Mongols for a hundred years. As a result, horse breeding operations were set up in various sites around the island. Unlike the Goryeo government, which saw little value in

---

ANTI-MONGOLIAN RESISTANCE SITE: A DISCOVERY

Hangpaduri Hangmong Historical Site is the location of an earthen fortress built in 1270 as part of a struggle against Mongolian invasion. The Three Elite Patrols, a rogue military combat unit from the mainland, overtook the island's armed forces upon arrival and were joined by local residents in their efforts. Nearby Pagunbong, a gently sloping *oreum*, was the site of their annihilation by Mongolian-Goryeo forces three years later.

Officially designated Local Monument No. 29, the historic site has long held world anthropological and cultural heritage value: the Three Elite Patrols also acted as a provisional government, the first of its kind. The ruins have been frequently visited, and restoration work was undertaken in 1978. Recently, archaeologists made a remarkable discovery: there are indications of a large palace at this location. While written historical records of same existed, no physical evidence had been discovered until now.

A prospecting survey conducted by the Jeju Institute of Archaeology in May 2011 unearthed approximately 100 relics, all from the 13th century, indicating a large residential structure built using techniques reflecting advances made in civil engineering during that era. A number of the pieces are made of celadon, owned at that time by the elite class of the Goryeo kingdom. Some of the stonework discovered indicates columns around the structure's center. The archeology institute has deemed the excavation "urgent," and the Cultural Heritage Administration of Korea has joined the effort, with a future restoration in the realm of possibility.

Several legends are associated with the area. The Jangsumul is a spring said to have emerged from the deep, giant footprints left by General Kim of the Three Elite Patrols as he leapt from the fortress wall to the ground. The purportedly medicinal spring was alleged to have been the source of Goseong villagers' resistance to a cholera outbreak that affected neighboring villages. Following that period, further legends characterized it as a spring of immortality.

Hangpaduri Hangmong Historical Site is located in Goseong Village, Aewol District, between Hallim District and Jeju City. Jeju Olle trail No. 16 passes the site.

the island, the Mongols showed an avid interest, regarding it as a forward base for their advance across the sea into Japan. With this in mind, the Mongols initiated a number of projects, including the construction of ships, the breeding of war horses, and the reconstruction of Beophwa Temple, all while attempting to construct a palace. At the Beophwa site in Seogwipo's Hawon district, tile shards and roof-end tiles bearing inscriptions of dragons and phoenixes have been excavated. Not far from the temple site, a tomb believed to belong to a descendant of the Mongolian leader Genghis Khan is currently being excavated.

JOSEON DYNASTY: EXILES AND REBELLIONS

During the Joseon Dynasty (1392–1910), the government was much more centralized than in the preceding Goryeo era, and Jeju Island was treated as a frontier region. Mainlanders tended to think of it not as the home of fellow citizens but as a faraway place where horses were bred and political prisoners exiled. To make matters worse, in the 17th century King Injo issued a royal edict that prohibited the islanders from entering the mainland. The edict remained in effect for 200 years until the early 19th century, reinforcing the complete isolation of the islanders.

During the Joseon era, the inhabitants of Jeju Island were sometimes referred to as *ryukgoyeok* ("the six hard labors"). The term meant that the islanders were engaged in six physically demanding occupations: diving for shellfish, constructing ports, herding livestock, maintaining fruit orchards, constructing boats, and cultivating rice. Among these workers were those responsible for gathering and delivering the abalone, mandarin oranges, horses, and medicinal herbs paid in tribute to the king. In order to meet the mandatory quotas, the islanders were forced to risk their lives diving into the deep waters off the coast and farming the high terraces of Mt. Halla.

For the beleaguered islanders, the sea was a barrier separating the island from the mainland. Facing such inhospitable conditions, they naturally developed a philosophy of life that was centered on basic survival. This philosophy can be found embodied in forms of collective labor such as *sunurum* (mutual aid) and in extreme frugality, as typified by the practice of *jonyang*.

Unwilling to endure the oppressive conditions, islanders rebelled against the central government on a number of occasions toward the end of the Joseon era. The 1862 Kang Je Geom Rebellion, the 1898 Bang Seong Chil Rebellion, and the 1901 Lee Jae Su Rebellion were large-scale uprisings of the common people that struck fear into the heart of the government. Through these movements, the people of Jeju Island fostered a spirit of direct defiance against nepotism and exploitation. In particular, the Lee Jae Su Rebellion, a struggle against corruption within the area's burgeoning Catholic

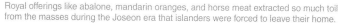

Royal offerings like abalone, mandarin oranges, and horse meat extracted so much toil from the masses during the Joseon era that islanders were forced to leave their home.

church, resulted in a stern response from France, which had led the missionary effort, and from other countries. A movie made about these events was given an international release, an indication that the incident was of great significance not only to Koreans but to the international community as well. Relics and sites associated with the incident include the plaza at Gwandeok Pavilion in Jeju City, the public Catholic cemetery at Hwangsapyeong in Jeju's Hwabuk district, the Inseong Village Town Fortress, and the Samuisabi (Monument of the Three Martyrs) in the northern part of the island. The last of these commemorates Lee Jae Su and two other leaders of the rebellion.

In addition, Jeju Island was a favored place for the banishment of political exiles. Members of the royal house (among them Prince Gwanghaegun) and high-ranking politicians found guilty of intrigue were banished to the island. Many of these people became important in later genealogical records as the first of their clan to live on Jeju Island. Some of the exiles were brilliant

The Uprising is a film based on the 1901 rebellion led by Lee Jae Su and Oh Dae-hyeon against the abuses of corrupt Catholics who wielded tremendous authority with the support of imperialist forces (top).

Samuisabi, the Monument of the Three Martyrs, honors the three leaders of the 1901 rebellion: Lee Jae Su, Gang U-baek, and Oh Dae-hyeon. The three of them voluntarily reported to the court only to face execution (bottom).

Event to reenact the Joseon era exile parade

scholars who had a profound influence on scholarship on the island. In particular, the islanders highly regarded Kim Chong (pen name Jung-am), Cheong On (pen name Dong-gye) and Song Si-yeol (pen name Woo-am). These scholars were part of the group of "Five Sages" venerated at Gyullim Seowon, a local Confucian school. At the former site of the school, which lies within Jeju's South Gate Fortress Site, is the Ohyeondan (Five Sages Shrine), housing a monument to commemorate these scholars.

In 1840, Kim Jeong-hui (pen name Chu-sa), a scholar famous for his philologico-biographical studies, was falsely accused of amid factional disputes and exiled to Jeju. During his eight years of exile,

With water surrounding them on all sides, exiled Joseon aristocrats and Confucian scholars spent their life not knowing if or when they would ever return. Many died alone here, in some cases producing brilliant works of art and literature amid their solitude.

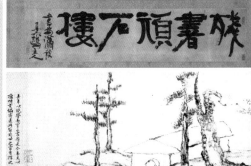

1. Kim Jeong-hui was a leading late Joseon calligrapher, epigrapher, and documental archaeologist who spent eight years in exile on Jeju Island.
2. During his exile, Kim created the Chu-sa Style of calligraphy while studying writing methods passed down to Joseon from the Three Kingdoms period. 3. *Sehando (Landscape in Winter)* is a National Treasure painted in 1844 by Kim Jeong-hui for a student visiting him on Jeju.

he lived at the home of Kang Do-sun at Daejeonghyeol in the southern part of the island. He had a significant influence on the area's young Confucian scholars, teaching a number of them his distinctive calligraphy style, which is known today as the "Chu-sa Style." Kim's famous work *Sehando (Landscape in Winter)* is said to have been painted during this period. The site of the house where he stayed is still preserved within Daejong District Fortress.

JAPANESE OCCUPATION AND RESISTANCE MOVEMENT

After Japan annexed Korea in 1910, the people of Jeju Island lived in poverty and hunger. In order to survive, many went to Japan to work under wretched conditions in mines and textile factories. In particular, many islanders relocated to Japan after the opening of a direct route between Jeju Island and Osaka in 1923.

| 1 | 2 |
| 3 | 4 |

1. A native of Waheul Village in Jeju City, Im Do-hyun (middle front) waged a campaign against Japan after escaping to China on a Japanese military plane. 2. Site of Beopjeong Temple in Seogwipo, the epicenter of Jeju's anti-Japanese movement during the occupation era. In October 1918, a group of 400 monks and other people opposed to Japanese rule gathered at the temple to launch their movement. 3. Japanese military hangar built on Jeju Island 4. Interior of a Japanese army cave stronghold at Sesal Oreum. Many islanders were arrested by the Japanese military and forced to dig tunnels.

During this oppressive period, the islanders were actively involved in the struggle against Japanese occupation. Following the 1919 independence demonstrations, young socialists led the island's anti-Japanese movement. From the formation of the Shininhoe (New People's Association) in 1925 to the mid-1930s when the movement was driven underground by Japanese suppression, these activists represented the mainstream of the province's struggle against colonialism. The peak of the movement came with the resistance of the island's diving women, which took place between 1931 and early 1932 in six villages in Gujwa and Seongsan Townships. It occurred when the women who earned a living diving for shellfish off the island's coast rose up against the heavy-handed actions of the Divers Association, which was overseen by the Japanese. About 17,000 people participated in the struggle, and over 100 were arrested in what would go down as the island's most notable anti-Japanese protest and Korea's largest protest ever led by women and people working in the fishing industry. The movement was quashed by harsh suppression from Japan, with local leaders conscripted into military service or forced to labor for the Japanese war effort.

In Jocheon Township, the islanders' anti-colonial movement is honored in the Jeju Anti-Japanese Memorial Museum. Some of the military facilities that the Japanese built on the island during World War II have been preserved as a further reminder of the suffering that the islanders endured. Examples include remnants of the Alduru Airport at Sangmo Village and remnants of cave fortifications on Mt. Songak along the coast.

APRIL 3RD UPRISING

With the country's liberation from Japanese colonial rule, the island and all of Korea came under the jurisdiction of the U.S. military government. A couple of years later, in 1947, more than ten islanders were injured or killed when police opened fire on them during the anniversary of the Independence Movement of March 1, 1919. As a show of protest, many of the island's public offices, schools, and other workplaces were closed in a general strike by their staff. The U.S. military government responded with a stern crackdown on demonstrators. In the year following the strike, approximately 2,500 people were arrested, and in March 1948

Gwandeok Pavilion. Here, the death or injury of more than people when police fired on civilians on March 1, 1947, touched off the April 3rd Uprising (left).
Jeongbang Falls at the time of the uprising. The building at the top of the frame is a button factory from the Japanese occupation. Many residents were held here before being massacred above the falls at the time of the uprising (right).

three incidents occurred in which people were killed during police interrogations.

In response to these events, some young Jeju inhabitants fled to the foot of Mt. Halla, where they prepared an armed revolt. These young people are said to have opposed elections for a distinct South Korean government, scheduled for May 10, 1948. Finally, in the early morning hours of April 3, 1948, armed units from this rebel group attacked 11 police stations throughout the island as well as the headquarters of various rightist organizations. This marked the beginning of the April 3rd Uprising.

In response, the U.S. military government, working in conjunction with the national military and local police forces, set out to subdue the "communist rebels" throughout the island. In the process, most mountain villages were burned down, and many law-abiding citizens were killed. During the short period from August 1948, when the government of South Korea was established, to the spring of 1949, thousands of people were persecuted and evacuation orders issued for residents of more than 130 villages. In the end, the island's society was utterly devastated.

It is impossible to estimate the number of cases in which innocent people were victimized in some manner. For example, the people of Dosan Village in Pyoseon Township were forced to move from a mountain village to the coast. On December 14, 1948, soldiers arrested the villagers, brought them to Pyoseon Beach, and killed 157 of them. In another incident on January 17, 1949, soldiers surrounded Bukchon Village in Jocheon Township, claiming that the residents had been colluding with communist rebels. They burned down over 300 houses and assembled the residents on the athletic field of an elementary school, where they proceeded to execute approximately 400 of them. It makes one shudder to contemplate the thousands of people who died in such a short time on such a small island.

The tragedy did not end there. When the Korean War began on June 25, 1950, many relatives of the armed rebels were placed under arrest and eventually executed at Jeju Airport, Sarabong, and other locations. Most of those in prison on the mainland for their part in the April 3rd Uprising were also summarily executed. The

Victims buried after the massacre at Jeongtteureu Airfield, which witnesses say was the largest of the uprising. Their remains were excavated and carried to burial by members of the association of surviving family members.

Cultural performance for the annual April 3rd Memorial Festival (left)
Gut ritual to soothe the spirits of those innocently sacrificed in the April 3rd Uprising (right)

132 people buried in Donggwang Village of Andeok Township were killed at this time. On August 20, 1950, those incarcerated at Moseulpo in the Daejong district were taken to a munitions dump on the north side of Mt. Songak and executed. When the bereaved family members found the mass grave seven years later, the bodies had deteriorated to such a degree that identification was impossible. The corpses were therefore placed together in a mass tomb, and a monument was erected with the inscription *Baekjoilsonjiji*—"Place of a Hundred Grandfathers and One Grandson."

For the people of Jeju Island, the April 3rd Uprising represents a horrific tragedy. While the circumstances of that era are complex and research insufficient, all parties agree that more than 85% of the killing was committed by the national and local security forces and that the "rebellion" was suppressed with a force now officially considered "excessive."

The islanders boast a history of survival and struggle against harsh natural conditions, but much of their culture was lost during that terrible time. In a sense, the incident can be seen as the final chapter of the island's history; following that time, there was strong political suppression and an effort by the military governments of the mainland to absorb Jeju into Korea once and for all. Islanders believe that the truth of that time must be fully brought to light so that Jeju can reclaim its history and regain its lost identity.

Many tourists who come to Jeju Island are entranced by its beautiful scenery and pristine environment. But few are aware of the tragic history that lingers on this small island.

Jeju Islanders carry the pain of their struggle as part of their character. They do not forget—but they are not a wounded people. Rather, they have developed a resistance to difficulty, a courage that rises to meet each challenge, and an indomitable spirit that has led the way from times of great hardship and deep sorrow to an era of prosperity. Today's "Jejudo-*saram*," or Jeju native, has inherited a DNA forged in the dual fires of labor and tragedy, emerging with a strength of will to be admired—and emulated.

The people of Jeju have the true power to smile brightly despite the ordeals of history and their difficult lives.

APRIL 3RD PEACE PARK AND MEMORIAL HALL

The April 3rd Peace Park and Memorial Hall was opened to the public and dedicated on April 3, 2008—sixty years after the original episode of violence for which it is named. Its founders and the people of Jeju have noted that the sixty-year span is a significant one in a tradition inherited from Ancient China. Specifically, based on the Chinese zodiac, it represents an identical alignment of the stars to the date 60 years earlier, indicating a closing of one chapter and the beginning of another.

As of April 7, 2011, the memorial hall had received more than 500,000 visitors. More than 10,000 people attended its April 3rd memorial service. Its website offers a feature for "cyber-worship," which permits the people of Jeju to remember their dead in a unique way.

The complex combines a wide range of facilities. Among them are the noted Peace Memorial Hall, which functions as a museum and gallery and houses a research department, and the All Souls Altar, the site of the annual service, within which a memorial wall with names of victims is housed. Additionally,

The April 3rd Peace Park and Memorial Hall, along with a chunk of the Berlin Wall donated by the city of Berlin as a symbol of peace

there is a memorial tower and shrine entitled "Returning to Heaven," another memorial hall that houses cremated remains in celadon urns and a recreation of a mass burial site, a graveyard, and numerous statues, along with other artwork and landscapes. Peace Park officials have plans for its expansion.

The work of many Jeju artists is on display in the Memorial Hall's permanent exhibit, among them renowned *Sa-sam* (April 3rd) artists Kang Yo-bae and Koh Gill-chun.

Special exhibits are shown for short periods in the second floor gallery. In April 2010, the drawings and writings of survivor Im Gyeong Jae were exhibited. At the age of 75, Im, a lifelong farmer, began spontaneously and prolifically producing artwork that represented a flood of memories from that era, suffering a stroke in the process.

This year's special exhibition was called *Lost Villages* and included photographs, artists' renderings, poetry, and testimony describing villages that were destroyed.

The Peace Park serves as a reminder that the historical trauma and its victims, the devastated villages, and the more than 60 years of efforts toward truth, reconciliation, and healing need to be transformed into a lasting example of peace. A portion of the Berlin Wall stands at the entry as further evidence of this need. The park and memorial hall are open to visitors daily.

Inside the April 3rd Peace Park and Memorial Hall (left)
Breastfeeding (2007) by Kang Yo-bae, a painter who depicted the April 3rd Uprising (right)

Chapter Five

ISLAND OF LONGEVITY

Each morning at 6am, the local park is filled with people. Some walk the trails up and down hills beneath 20-meter-tall pine trees. Others hug a tree, tapping their body against its trunk repeatedly. Many utilize the area's exercise equipment. Some lift weights, others jog. Still more walk barefoot down the long path of small stones, stimulating reflex zones on the soles of their feet for the health of the whole body. They are silent, contemplative, and meditative, breathing slowly and deeply.

All are over 60 years of age—many of them by a decade or two.

At midday in the gazebo at the top of the park's hill, a dozen elderly women sit and chat. Or nap. Or pet the dog that one of them inevitably brings. They are there every day, spending their afternoons under the trees, in the company of one another. Children soon flood into the nearby playground, filling the air with their laughter and shouts of sheer delight

Jeju's long-lived people

Jeju is well known for its long-lived people. Ranked first among Korean provinces for longevity, with 65 centenarians currently documented in a population of just over half a million, the island first began keeping such records in 1704. Nearly two millennia prior, according to legend, this island was imagined far and wide, even by the emperor of China, to house the elixir of eternal life— undoubtedly the result of a reputation within the region for longevity even then.

A 91-year-old man in a village on the southern shore lives alone in the customized house he built for the storage of grain more than 50 years ago, when he was also the village chief. He has written two books and is an expert on his village's history—"Our village is more than a thousand years old, but I only really know the past four hundred," he says—and spends his days reading and chatting with

The elderly women of Jeju engage in vibrant interaction that belies their advanced years.

visitors. He needs only reading glasses and has all his teeth, keen hearing, a full head of thick white hair, and a sharp mind, though he describes himself as "an uneducated man."

He is also the only remaining official skills holder for the "Rice Harvest Song," used during labor in this rare village that, thanks to its underground springs, was able to grow the prized grain.

"Blue Zones" are areas around the globe where inhabitants typically reach an advanced age while maintaining relative health and an active lifestyle. Jeju has not yet been added to the official list, unlike the nearby island of Okinawa. Nevertheless, it shares many of the common characteristics found in these regions: family and community connectedness, social engagement and a sense of purpose, regular physical activity, and a diet that is primarily plant-

Jeju islanders work hard well into their old age.

based, regularly includes whole grains and legumes, and is consumed in small quantities.

To prepare for the inevitable aging of its population, the central government of Korea recently launched a "centenarian project" that aims to support senior citizens' social engagement and independence—characteristics that have traditionally defined the elders of Jeju.

The vibrant 78-year-old woman in the apartment above lives alone, doing her gardening and visiting her neighbors each day. She has lived in this "village" within Jeju City—in fact, the same apartment over this house—for the past 25 years.

Another woman of equal or greater age passes through the streets each day, bent over and pushing a heavy cart as she collects cardboard for recycling—and the meager remuneration she receives in return.

The women of "Arirang Kimchi," a small enterprise in a western farming village, decided that retirement didn't suit them. Joining together, they began producing and distributing their handmade kimchi from a farm storeroom converted into a commercial kitchen. These women meet and work together five full days a week—and they range in age from their mid-sixties to early eighties.

Shin Chang-hyun, who turned 72 in 2011, is a skill holder of the *heobeokjang*, a Jeju Island Intangible Cultural Property. He is still highly active in the art.

The people of Jeju are well known for their strong spirit; unlike their mainland counterparts, senior citizens on Jeju make every effort not to depend upon family members, but to maintain their independent status and lifestyle, including their professional work and income, for as long as possible. While a source of hardship, lifelong communal labor has provided both physical activity and shared purpose. Regular hiking of Mt. Halla and the island's nearly 400 *oreum*, long a tradition among Jeju's inhabitants, adds to their physical prowess.

The diving women, dwindling in number because their daughters and granddaughters now want office jobs, are typically over sixty. Some are much older. Some even dive in their nineties. Though difficult and dangerous work, the diving gives them purpose, meaning, and economic independence and freedom. It is also communal: the women share the work, the proceeds, the business aspects, and their lives as they regularly converse as a group before

and after the actual diving. And there are hidden benefits as well.

"When I'm in the water," one says, "I think of nothing but the catch before me. And when I come out of the water, all my worries and cares have disappeared."

Another key feature of the Jeju people's health and longevity is their deeply felt connection to the natural environment. Extensive research has shown that regular interaction with nature contributes to mental, emotional, and physical well-being. The Jeju natives, with their animistic tradition now referred to as "shamanism," have traditionally viewed nature in a spiritual manner, making this the "island of 18,000 gods."

1		5
2	4	
3		6

Jeju residents work hard together. Among the things contributing to their long lifespans are economic independence and freedom, as well as a clear goal in life.
1. Jeju women gather to talk and shell garlic cloves.
2. An elderly Jeju man making bamboo baskets
3. Jeju men working in an orchard
4. Diving women keep working through to the end of their lives.
5. After working together under the same conditions, diving women check their catch.
6. The *bulteok* is where diving women talk about their lives with others.

"To understand Jeju, you must first understand this: Halla is our mother, and the *oreum* are our sisters."

An eastern seaside community center is filled with a hundred elderly women, all talking at once and sharing food as they look forward to an annual shamanic ritual known as the *jamsu* gut. These *jamsu*—diving women, also known as *haenyeo*—are contributing to personal and societal longevity in profound ways.

The *jamsu gut* (top). The women of the coast carefully prepare fruit and other dishes to wish for a year of well-being and good fortune (bottom).

The village structure of Jeju has encouraged social activities, rituals for seasonal and life passages, and a sense of belonging and engagement. Furthermore, within each small village there can be found an intricately interdependent system of relationship known as *gwendang*, which contributes to a profound experience of community and security, and a philosophy of *sunurum*, or mutual aid.

In a western farming village, a hundred elderly women and men gather for a ceremony of recognition and a communal meal to celebrate Parents' Day. In accordance with Confucian tradition, village leaders and provincial council members bow to their elders as a means of honoring them.

The island culture is also known for its particularly pure mineral water, fresh air, and healthy food. Jeju's cuisine was once considered secondary to that of the mainland: it depended on whole grains, which were thought of as food fit only for livestock and grown because the rocky soil and drought conditions did not permit rice to thrive, and the food was relatively scarce due to impoverishment and harsh growing conditions. Today, however, is renowned for its healthful properties.

The people of Jeju perform village tasks together, each helping the others. As a result, the working song has flourished. These residents at a festival are reenacting the "Gotbaguri Well-Digging Song," which tells of the hard lot of working together to make large buckets owing to the village's lack of artesian wells.

THE LEGEND OF XU FU:
SEEKING THE ELIXIR OF LIFE

Xu Fu, court sorcerer for Emperor Qin Shi Huang, was sent to Mt. Halla to find the elixir of life. He is said to have left this inscription on the rock face of Jeongbang Falls reading "Xu Fu passed by here."

There is a local legend regarding an emperor of ancient China, Qin Shi Huang (259–210 B.C.). It tells of the court sorcerer Xu Fu (called Seo Bok in Korean), who was dispatched by the emperor to find the elixir of life at Mt. Yeongju (an early name for Mt. Halla), one of the three sacred mountains where the immortals were said to live.

In order to comply with the emperor's orders, the legend says, Xu climbed up Mt. Yeongju with thousands of boys and girls in search of the elixir. When he arrived at Jeongbang Falls, he was so captivated by its beauty that he carved the words "Xu Fu passed by here" in the rock face before heading west. The name of Seogwipo is said to derive from this inscription.

The legendary quest for longevity lives on today in the discipline of "brain art meditation." Every year, some 3,000 visitors from places such as the United States, Canada, Japan, Germany, Russia, and Hong Kong come to

The Xu Fu Gallery in Seogwipo (left). A monument bearing an inscription
in the handwriting of Chinese Premier Wen Jiabao at Xu Fu Park (right)

experience a meditative journey that has been led for the past ten years by
Lee Ilchi, president of the Korea Institute of Brain Science (KIBS), at the
Health and Longevity Theme Park of the Jeju Korean History and Culture Park.

Brain art meditation involves traditional Korean meditation and health
practices, such as *gi* exercises and hypogastric breathing. The goal is to
discover oneself and heal one's mind. Lee believes in the legend of Xu Fu and
the long-sought elixir of longevity.

It is thought that the elixir of life that Xu was looking for is derived from the
Korean dendropanax tree *(Dendropanax morbifera)*, which is said to contain
a pharmacological agent effective in combatting aging.

The Xu Fu Gallery, opened in 2003 above the western cliff of Jeongbang
Falls, is rooted in the legend of Xu's exploits. At the entrance, a stone
monument bears the words "Xu Fu Park," carved from characters written by
Chinese Premier Wen Jiabao.

EXPLORING JEJU'S SAVORY DELICACIES

A perception that the island's cuisine might have something to do with the longevity of its population has led to a spotlighting of the health benefits and wholesome influence of Jeju's food culture.

Seafood dominates many of the dishes for which Jeju Island is noted and colors a food culture that sets itself apart from that of the Korean mainland. Fresh, glistening, near-translucent slices of *hoe* (raw fish or sashimi), cut from fish that have just been caught, are a must for any gourmand, as are stews chock full of abalone and bubbling with various other fruits of the sea in earthen pots known as *obunjagi haemul ttukbaegi*.

Grilled *okdom* (red tilefish) and *galchi* (large-head hairtail) melt like butter on the palate. The long, silvery, cutlass-like *galchi* is another soup favorite. A seaweed known as *mojaban (Sargassum fulvellum)* is served up in a pork broth called *momguk*. Sea urchin also brings a salty tang when included in soup dishes.

1. Grilled Jeju black pig 2. Mandarin oranges, a Jeju specialty. 3. *Hoe*

Jeju's Water

Water has always been scarce on Jeju, which sits on porous layers of basalt. The earthenware water jars exhibited at the Folklore and Natural History Museum are symbolic of the hardship endured by local women, who used them to draw water from artesian springs. The underground water that so vexed the women of Jeju in the past is now a valuable resource that has given birth to a thriving water industry. The Jeju SamDaSoo brand of aquifer water is the island's answer to Evian.

Jeju Governor Woo Keun-min offers his guests SamDaSoo water rather than coffee or tea. "SamDaSoo is pumped up from 420 meters below the surface," he has said. "Rain that falls on Mt. Halla passes through dozens of layers of volcanic basalt to finally reach the water table, a journey that takes over 18 years." Every day, the SamDaSoo plant in Jeju City processes up to 2,100 tons of water that has passed inspection by the U.S. Federal Department of Agriculture and Japan's Ministry of Health, Labor and Welfare. This water is exported to the U.S., China, Japan, and Indonesia. It is refreshing and slightly alkaline, containing naturally occurring minerals.

"Jeju's mineral water is of world-class quality," Woo says. "We have plans to create a water industry cluster that includes a hydrotherapy center and producers of specialty liquors, health drinks, and cosmetics."

Those uninitiated to the world of "water *hoe*" would do well to try out this Jeju Island specialty by simply dipping their chopsticks into a bowl filled with tender, succulent slices of raw *jaridom* (pearlspot chromis, a delicious small fish that resembles sea bream) or *hanchi* (miniature mitra squid) sitting in a bath of spicy, savory, ice-cold broth.

Obunjagi Ttukbaegi

For those unfamiliar with the classic dish known as *obunjagi ttukbaegi*, it is made with small abalone (*obunjagi*) that is found clinging to rocks 20 meters under the water. Seventy percent of the nation's *obunjagi* is supplied by Jeju Island.

Horned or spiny turban shells—like ocean varieties of escargot—are added along with shrimp and clams to a stew seasoned with *doenjang* (soybean paste) and *gochujang* (red pepper paste) to yield a distinctly piquant and refreshing flavor.

These soups are often accompanied by *bingtteok*, an incredibly flavorful local dish made from a buckwheat crepe filled with finely sliced, blanched, and seasoned daikon radish.

Black Barley Noodles

Culinary nostalgia is very much in fashion these days as a focus on healthy living has sparked interest in reviving long-cherished flavors of traditional fare lovingly prepared by the grandmothers and ancestors of modern-day Koreans.

At the Black Barley Noodle restaurant in Jeju City's Ildo 2-dong neighborhood, proprietor Kim Jeong-ja was inspired by fond memories of her grandmother's tasty black barley pancakes. Kim used black barley rice as the primary ingredient in developing her signature *pajeon* (green onion pancake), *sujebi* (hand-torn dough served in a soup), and noodles.

"The black barley harvest yields much less than with regular barley, but it has this wonderful fragrance," Kim says. "It boasts over five times as much fiber as regular barley and is rich in iron, phosphorus, potassium, and other minerals, making it helpful in preventing diseases."

When Kim prepares her barley rice batter, she combines ground potatoes, mountain yam, and mushrooms with water to create a springy texture. For her noodle soup, she makes a clean-tasting, light broth from kelp, anchovies, and salt. Sea gastropods, another Jeju Island delicacy, impart a refreshing, clean flavor to her *sujebi* soup.

Horse Meat Delicacies

When it comes to meat, Jeju Island is known for its pheasant, pork from the black pig, and, last but not least, *malgogi*, or horse meat delicacies.

In the past, Korea's horses were bred and raised on Jeju Island, leading to an abundance of the animals and the development of dishes from their meat. During the Joseon Dynasty, it is said, horse was presented alongside abalone and mandarin oranges as a local tribute to the royal court. This means that it was likely served as part of the king's *sura*, or main meals.

Horse, however, was not restricted to royalty alone; common people dined on the meat as well. It was consumed after the tenth

month of the lunar calendar, when the meat was less gamey. Since the meat has so little fat on it, it was enjoyed as tartare and braised short ribs or served seasoned and grilled. The bones were used to make broth or ground into a powder to treat neuralgia.

Horse meat started to appear on restaurant menus in the 1980s, when tourists began flocking to the island in search of the delicacy. There are currently more than 40 restaurants on Jeju that serve horse dishes.

Mandarin Orange Coffee and Chocolate

The mandarin orange is Jeju Island's number one fruit product. The sweet, tasty fruit is grown on the island's numerous mandarin orange farms. Over 20 varieties of the juicy citrus have been developed, including the popular Hallabong and Cheonhyehyang, premium fruits sold at supermarkets throughout the country.

Mandarin oranges are also used to flavor chocolate and *makgeolli*, a traditional rice wine that is currently enjoying a resurgence among trendsetters. The fruit's peel is used as a medicinal ingredient, too. For instance, the peel of the *jin* variety of mandarin orange can be boiled in water to make a decoction for treating digestive ailments, while *cheong* peel is used for medication to treat malaria and bacterial diseases.

JEJU FOOD CULTURE

Visitors can learn about the local cuisine of Jeju Island at the Folklore and Natural History Museum of the Jeju Special Self-Governing Province. Because island life was so basic in the past, food was an especially precious thing. Furthermore, cooking methods had to be simple, since most women worked as divers or farmers and did not have much time for household chores.

Hence, dishes based on raw ingredients were favored over those

1. Recreation of a Joseon era meal. This healthful menu consists of multigrain rice, vegetables, and grilled fish. 2. Young rape flower shoots paint Jeju yellow in the spring. They can be prepared and eaten, and their fruit is pressed for oil. Rape flower sprouts are a healthy food rich in Vitamin C. 3. An organic green tea farm using manure from free-range livestock as fertilizer 4. Jeju carrots are popular for their juiciness and sweet flavor.

that required time-consuming steaming, boiling, or simmering. As a result, the cuisine of the island has highlighted the natural flavors of the ingredients rather than the seasonings, resulting in the distinctive characteristics of Jeju's local food culture.

The perception that the island's cuisine might have something to do with the longevity of its population has led to the spotlighting of the health benefits and wholesome influence of Jeju's food culture. People have become more aware of its primary ingredients, which come from the clean ocean waters and fields nearby, and the fact that the fast cooking methods minimize the loss of nutrients.

Hyeon Hak-su, a public relations official at the Jeju Provincial Government, says, "We have plans to highlight over 470 kinds of Jeju Island cuisine that are good for your health and longevity."

REPRESENTATIVE FOODS OF JEJU: A GUIDE

- **Bingtteok**: Cold buckwheat crepes filled with daikon radish (julienned, blanched, and marinated)
- **Galchi**: Largehead hairtail, served grilled, boiled in a spicy stew, raw, or in *mulhoe* (see below)
- **Galchi Hobak-guk**: Hairtail fish and pumpkin stew
- **Godeungeo**: Mackerel, served grilled or raw
- **Gusal-guk**: Sea urchin roe and seaweed soup
- **Heuk Dwoeji**: Pork from the black pig. This meat has a mild flavor and is served in slices, grilled or boiled.
- **Hoe**: Any type of raw fish or shellfish; this is a very common dish, with a wide variety of seafood served.
- **Jeonbok**: Abalone, served in *juk* (porridge), as *jang* (stir-fried on the half shell), or raw
- **Kkwong**: Pheasant, served in dumplings, with buckwheat noodles and vegetables, or blanched in "shabu-shabu" style (stew); also made into a sweet "taffy" (spread/dip)
- **Memil**: Buckwheat, used in making *kalguksu* (noodle soup), mandu (dumplings), *beombeok* (thick porridge with other grains), and other dishes
- **Momguk**: Pork soup with vegetables and seaweed; also known as *mojaban* soup
- **Mulhoe**: A spicy cold broth with raw fish. Its name literally means "water raw." Common variations use *galchi*, *jari* (perch), or *hanchi* (cuttlefish).
- **Myeolchi-jeot**: Pickled anchovies, served as a side dish or condiment
- **Okdom**: Tilefish, served broiled, grilled, raw, or in a stew

1. *Bingtteok* 2. Grilled hairtail, hairtail and pumpkin stew
3. Grilled mackerel 4. Raw mackerel 5. Grilled *okdom*
6. Pheasant dishes 7. Grilled abalone and abalone porridge
8. *Momguk* pork stew 9. *Mulhoe*

1	2	3
4	5	6
7	8	9

Traditionally, the most common meal on Jeju was *japgokbap* (a bowl of steamed mixed grains including buckwheat, millet, and barley) with *jaban* (fish of different varieties preserved with salt) and a soup with a *doenjang* (fermented soybean paste) base.

One of the primary crops today is the *gamgyul*, a small variety of mandarin orange or tangerine. The Hallabong, a larger citrus similar to the navel orange, is also commonly grown.

When on Jeju, be sure to look for restaurants bearing the name "Haenyeo-aejip," or "Diving Woman House." These will offer the freshest seafood. When buying food-related products, don't miss a visit to one of the *oiljang*, the traditional open-air markets held every five days.

Conclusion

"Free International City"

Jeju Island is undergoing change, quietly but steadily. Like blossoming flowers, structures designed by world-class architects have emerged along the 258 kilometers of the island's coastline, with attention given to harmonizing architecture with Jeju's natural environment. Phoenix Island in Seogwipo is home to Club House Agora by the master of geometric architecture, Mario Botta, and Glass House and Genius Loci by Tadao Ando, who favors a minimalist style. Jun Itami's Stone Art Gallery, Wind Art Gallery, Church of Sky, and Podo Hotel can be seen on other areas of the shore. The North London Collegiate School Jeju—part of the Jeju

Genius Loci, built on Seogwipo's Phoenix Island by world-renowned architect Tadao Ando

Global Education City, which is scheduled to begin classes in September—was also designed by Itami.

Jeju Global Education City is an ambitious project that local authorities are actively pursuing, along with the development of the local medicine and health care industry and several other grand initiatives. By 2015, plans call for the completion of 12 international schools, an English education center, and related facilities in an area of Seogwipo, a project that is designed to ultimately attract a population of 30,000. It has been confirmed that England's North London Collegiate School and Canada's Branksome Hall will be operating schools here.

Jeju is also fostering its MICE (meetings, incentives, conferencing, and exhibitions) industry with the aim of becoming one of the top 25 international convention destinations in the world. "Jeju Island has hosted the 2009 ASEAN Summit, the 2010 China-Japan-Korea Summit, and a dozen other summit-level meetings, along with a total of 147 international conferences last year," noted governor

Completed in 2009, Saeyeon Bridge was modeled on the *teu*, the traditional Jeju boat.

Woo Keun-min.

The 2012 World Conservation Congress is also scheduled to be held on Jeju. Some 10,000 participants, including international environmental experts and political leaders, will meet to discuss the global environment.

"If you visit the Grand Canyon, you simply see an awesome natural spectacle, and only a chosen few can climb up and witness the beauty of Mt. Kilimanjaro," said Woo. "But on Jeju Island, anyone can experience the culture and beauty of our picturesque natural setting and feel the beauty of nature in the lives of the local people."

The provincial government's slogan is "The World Comes to Jeju, and Jeju Goes to the World." Indeed, Jeju is open to the world, with its many charms on offer.

OTHER INFORMATION

Facts about Jeju Island

- **Population:** 568,000, or 1.3% of South Korean total (2010)
- **Area:** 1,848km², or 1.85% of South Korean total
- **Political Units:** Two cities, seven towns, five districts, 31 neighborhoods
- **Land:** 48.1% forest/field, 20% dry paddy, 8.9% orchard, 8.9% pasture, 3% urban, 10.7% other
- **Colors:** Black (for the basalt predominant on Jeju), blue (for both the island's clean drinking water and its sea water), green (for the natural environment), and orange (for the hope of the people)

Jeju City Area

Seogwipo City Area

PROVINCIAL SYMBOLS

- **Tree:** Camphor tree (*Cinnamomum camphora*), representing "the enduring and indefatigable spirit of the Jeju people who, over the course of their history, have had to overcome great difficulties."
- **Bird:** The white-backed woodpecker (*Dendrocopos ieucotos*), which "lives in broadleaf forests and feeds on harmful insects."
- **Flower:** Rhododendron (*Rhododendron schlippenbachii*), in which "the harmony of the green leaves and red flowers symbolizes the ambitions and vitality of the Jeju people."

Jeju City

- **Population:** 414,000 (2010)
- **Location:** 16 kilometers north of Mt. Halla, 452 kilometers south of Seoul, 143 kilometers south of Mokpo, 291 kilometers southwest of Busan, 361 kilometers west of Fukuoka, Japan
- **Average Elevation:** 46 meters
- **Sister Cities:** Rouen, France; Adelaide, Australia; Brisbane, Australia; Beppu, Japan; Santa Rosa, California, USA; Shanghai, China; and more In 2009, 6,885,000 people visited tourist destinations in Jeju City.

Seogwipo City

- **Population:** 154,000 (2010)
- **Average Elevation:** 51 meters
- **Sister City:** Karatsu, Japan. In 2009, 11,450,000 people visited tourist destinations in Seogwipo.

Sources: Wolfram Alpha; Jeju Statistical Yearbook 2010

10 Most Beautiful Scenic Views of Jeju

1

Gosumongma
Yonggang-dong, Jeju-si

Herds of horses roaming freely in the foothills

2

Gyullimchusaek
Jeju-si

Old mandarin orchards around Ohyeondan Shrine

3

Jeongbang Falls
Donghong-dong, Seogwipo-si

Seaside waterfalls

4

Nokdam-manseol

Snow on top of Mt. Halla / in crater at Baengnokdam

5

Sabongnakjo
Jeju-si

Sunset over the sea as viewed from the peak of Sarabong

6

8

6

Sanbang Cave Buddhist Temple

Sagye-ri, Andeok-myeon, Seogwipo-si

Buddhist statue enshrined in a cave on southwest slope of Mt. Sanbang

7

Sanpojo-eo

Sight of fishing boats, white herons, and seagulls — the typical view from a fisherman's boat

8

Seongsan Ilchulbong (Sunrise Peak)

Seongsan-ri, Seongsan-eup, Seogwipo-si

View from a crater of sunrise at sea

9

Yeong-guchunhwa

Bangseonmun area of Odeung-dong

Azaleas in springtime bloom on Hallasan trail.

10

Yeongsil-giam

Hawon-dong, Seogwipo-si

Yeongsil Trail on Mt. Halla, with a formation of 500 rock pillars

What to do on Jeju Island: A "Bakers' Dozen"

❶ Hike to the top of **Mt. Halla** and picnic next to **Baengnokdam**.

❷ Climb an *oreum* (Recommended: Abu, Darangshi, Wollangbong, Saebyeol, Sarabong, Yongnuni).

❸ Walk an **Olle trail.** (Recommended: No. 7 or 8; also visit Yakcheon Temple en route)

❹ Visit **Geomun Oreum** (UNESCO site!) and explore **Manjang Cave**, the world's longest lava tube.

❺ Visit the **Haenyeo Museum** to learn about Jeju's legendary diving women.

❻ Learn about Jeju's tragic history, at **April 3rd Peace Park / Memorial Hall.**

❼ Explore the unique **Jeju Stone Park**—and stay in a **traditional village guesthouse**!

❽ **Ride** along the **Ring Road (Costal Roads)** by car, bicycle, scooter, or bus.

❾ View the sunrise from the crater of **Seongsan Ilchulbong**—and the sunset from Jeju City's **Sarabong**.

❿ Take a walk through the ancient **Bijarim Forest**, with its unique nutmeg grove.

⓫ Shop (and bargain!) at a **traditional, open-air fifth-day market**, which can be found in Jeju City, Seogwipo, and elsewhere.

⓬ Go swimming, strolling, or picnicking at any of **Jeju's beautiful beaches.** (Recommended: Gimnyeong, Hamdeok, Hamo, Hyeopjae, Jungmun, or Pyoseon)

AND:

Visit the outlying island of Udo for its special sights:

1. Fishing boats at night
2. Mt. Halla
3. Udo Beach from the peak of its *oreum*
4. Udo seen from the sea when approached by boat
5. The cliffs of Udo
6. Whale cave of the East Sea
7. The white red algae (not coral!) beach
8. The "Day Moon"—sunshine on an inner cave ceiling every day at noon.
9. AND: Olle trail No. 1.1 around the island!

Jeju Dialect: "Jeju-eo"

Phrases in Jeju Dialect	Translation
GREETINGS	
Honjeoopseoye	Welcome, please come in.
Bangapsuda	Hello; goodbye; nice to meet you.
Gomapsuda	Thank you
Nalbopseo, issukwa?	Hello, are you there?
Eotteong sara jeomsukkwa? Penan haesukkwa?	How's life? Are you all right / comfortable?
Pokssak sogassuda	You did a great job! Well done!

IN A RESTAURANT OR SHOP	
Honjeo wang meogupseo	Please come and eat.
Hayeong jupseoye	Please give me more.
Hayeong popseo, dashi okudayang	Good luck with your sales; I'll come again.
Maendorong hontte hororog duryeo ssa bupsseo.	Please eat before it gets cold.
Matjosudage	It is delicious.
Anture dureo wang, jeonyeog meogeong gabseo	Please come in and have dinner.
Igeo eolmawukwa	How much is it?

OTHER USEFUL PHRASES	
Naga hakuda	I will do it.
Eodure gamsukkwa?	Where are you going?
Jejuen chom jongeo hawuda	There are a lot of interesting things to do on Jeju Island.
Hokkomman isibseoge	Please wait for a while.
Yeogiseo Seouldeore jeonhwa haezibjuyang?	Can I make a call to Seoul from here?
Sanyiyeong badayiyeong monttag jounge massum	Both the mountain and the sea are very nice.
Chommallo josuda	It is really good.
Musin geoyen goram shindi mollukuge?	You didn't understand what I said, did you?
Musing geol mongkaemikkwa? Honja opseoge.	Why are you so slow? Come quickly.
Neuyeong nayeong duridungshil soranghoge massim.	Let's be friends.

Books and Online Resources

Books

• **On Diving Women:**
Brenda Paik Sunoo, *Moon Tides: Jeju Island Grannies of the Sea*. Seoul: Seoul Selection, 2011.

• **On April 3rd Uprising:**
Hyun Ki Young, *Aunt Suni*. Seoul: Gak (1979; translation 2008)
Kim Sok Pom, *The Curious Tale of Mandogi's Ghost*. New York: Columbia University Press, 2010
Hyun Kil-Un, *Dead Silence and Other Stories of the Jeju Massacre*, Norwalk: EastBridge, 2006.

Articles

• **On Diving Women**
Gwon Gwi-Sook, "Changing Labor Processes of Women's Work: The Haenyeo of Jeju Island": *Korean Studies*, Volume 29, 2005.

• **On April 3rd Uprising Trauma**
Kwon Heonik, "Healing the Wounds of War: New Ancestral Shrines in Korea": *The Asia-Pacific Journal: Japan Focus*, 2009.

• **On Shamanism**
Timothy R. Tangherlini and Park So Young, "The Comings and Goings of a Korean Grandfather: The Yŏngdŭng Kut Sequence of a Cheju Island Village": *Korean Studies*, Volume 14, 1990.

WEBSITES

- **Jeju's New 7 Wonders of Nature Campaign:** www.jejun7w.com
- **Jeju Bioreserve:** www.unesco.org
- **Jeju World Natural Heritage:** http://jejuwnh.jeju.go.kr
- **Jeju Geopark:** http://geopark.nowenter.co.kr
- **SmartGrid: Jeju Testbed:** www.smartgrid.or.kr
- **Ieodo Ocean Research Facility:** http://ieodo.nori.go.kr
- **Jeju Government (lots of useful information about Jeju!):** http://english.jeju.go.kr
- **Jeju Provincial Tourism Association:** www.hijeju.or.kr
- **Bus Information:** http://bus.jeju.go.kr
- **Ferries:** www.visitkorea.or.kr
- **Homestays, Pensions and Other Accommodations:** http://jejudohomestay.com
- **Guesthouses:** www.gojejuguesthouse.com
- **Ecotour:** http://jejueco.com
- **Jeju Olle:** www.jejuolle.org
- *Gotjawal*: http://jeju.us
- **Hallim Park:** http://hallimpark.co.kr
- **Jeju Stone Park:** http://jejustonepark.com
- **Spirited Garden:** http://eng.spiritedgarden.com
- **Yeomiji Botanical Garden:** www.yeomiji.or.kr
- **Jeju Observatory [Korean only]:** http://star.jejusi.go.kr
- **Guide to Jeju Beaches:** www.jejuweekly.com
- **"Chilmeori *dang* Yeongdeung *gut*" ritual:** www.unesco.org
- **April 3rd Peace Park & Memorial Hall:** http://jeju43.jeju.go.kr
- **Jeju Peace Institute:** http://jpi.or.kr
- **Jeju Weekly (newspaper):** www.jejuweekly.com
- **Jeju Life (online magazine):** http://jejulife.net
- **KCTV-Jeju (English news):** www.kctvjeju.com
- **Arirang Radio: *"All That Jeju"*:** www.arirang.co.kr
- **Lost on Jeju (blog):** http://lostonjeju.blogspot.com
- **RhymesWithJeju (community group, Yahoo):** http://groups.yahoo.com

NOTE: Unless marked, the Korean-language sites will have an "English" button allowing visitors to view English-language versions.

The content of this book has been compiled, edited, and supplemented by Anne Hilty from the following articles published in:

Koreana, Vol. 13 No.2, Summer 1999

"Island of wind: A History of Misfortune, Banishment, and Suffering" by Park Chan-sik
"The Life and History of Cheju Women" by Han Rim-hwa

Koreana Vol. 25 No.2, Summer 2011

"Born of Volcanic Lava The Rapture and Sorrow of Jeju Island" by Heo Yeong-seon
"Jeju: The Past, Present and Future" by Choi Sung-ja
"Praying for the Mercy of the Goddess of Wind: Yeongdeung Shaman Rites" by Kim Yoo-kyung
"Legendary Strength of Jeju Women" by Heo Yeong-seon
"In Search of the Jeju Horse" by Kim Yoo-kyung
"Exploring Jeju's Savory Delicacies" by Choi Sung-ja

Introduction, Chapter 2, part of Chapter 5, and Conclusion were newly written by Anne Hilty.

PHOTOGRAPHS

Jeju Special Self-Governing Province 5, 6, 8, 11, 12, 13, 15, 19, 22, 24, 25, 26, 27, 28, 31, 34, 42, 43, 45, 46, 47, 49, 51, 54, 55, 56, 60, 62, 63, 68, 71, 74, 87, 88, 89, 90, 94, 105, 110, 112, 121, 127, 129, 134, 135, 141

Korea Tourism Organization 14, 17, 18, 19, 20, 21, 28, 32, 34, 35, 37, 40, 41, 45, 54, 70, 82, 91, 118, 119, 125

YonhapNews 23, 31, 41, 45, 50, 52, 53, 54, 57, 58, 59, 62, 63, 69, 70, 72, 73, 75, 77, 78, 80, 85, 88, 91, 96, 97, 98, 99, 100, 103, 106, 107, 111, 112, 115, 116, 117, 123, 130

Image Today 118, 125

Kim Young Gap Gallery Dumoak 16

Phoenix Island 126

Brenda Paik Sunoo 65, 67, 70, 72, 98, 104, 105, 109, 112, 113, 114

Jang Woo-jung 47, 66, 90, 120

Shin Yong-man 52, 53

CREDITS

Publisher	Kim Hyung-geun
Writer	Anne Hilty
Editor	Jang Woo-jung
Copy Editor	Colin A. Mouat
Proofreader	Ben Jackson
Designer	Jung Hyun-young